T0361717

PRESENTED TO

....

BY

....

ON THE OCCASION OF

....

DATE

....

THE OUTDOOR ADVENTURE DEVOTIONAL

THE OUTDOOR ADVENTURE DEVOTIONAL

ISBN 979-8-89151-060-9

Published by Barbour Publishing, Inc., 1810 Barbour Drive, Uhrichsville, Ohio 44683, www.barbourbooks.com

Our mission is to inspire the world with the life-changing message of the Bible.

Printed in China.

BOAST IN THE LORD ALONE

May the Lord silence all flattering lips
and every boastful tongue.
PSALM 12:3 NIV

God can use anything to illustrate biblical truth, including a day of fishing with your friends.

You know that some fishermen are notorious for their bragging. Who hasn't heard a particularly boastful angler talking with pride after catching the most fish—and the biggest one of the day?

The humble angler, on the other hand—the one most of us enjoy fishing with—is the guy who loves seeing others enjoy similar success. It's the one who realizes that everything, even a successful day of fishing, is a gift from God.

Remember that there's no better day of fishing than the

one in which everyone comes out grateful. . .grateful to God for the beauty of nature, for friendship, and for successes enjoyed. Let's never forget the apostle Paul's teaching, "But 'he who boasts, let him boast in the Lord'" (2 Corinthians 10:17 SKJV).

FOR FURTHER THOUGHT

How easy is it for you to cheer for your fellow adventurers? Why?

When have you put aside your own success to help someone else succeed? How did that go?

PRAYER

Father, may I never forget that any success I enjoy is Your gift to me. May I boast only in You.

REACH FOR THE JOY

"We must go through many hardships to enter the kingdom of God," they said.
ACTS 14:22 NIV

There's a feeling that mountain climbers get when they step onto a summit they never thought they'd reach. Bicyclists get the same sensation when they push through exhaustion to a point where they feel they could pedal all day. Sailors feel joy when they pass through the discomforts of being cold and wet to become one with the wind.

We've all had our own version of that incredible feeling. You know when and how it happened, but the words to describe it probably fail you. These are the moments we rise above this world and briefly touch a joy beyond our understanding.

This is the reason we seek adventure in God's creation. But never forget that heaven will be better by far than even our most exhilarating moments on this earth. And for those moments that are anything but exhilarating? Well, it's great to know that the hardships we face now will be completely forgotten in the perfection of eternity.

FOR FURTHER THOUGHT

What about heaven intrigues you the most? What is most mysterious to you?

How can you remind yourself that what you experience in heaven will be worth the hardships of earth?

PRAYER

Father, I know the road to heaven is a tough one. In my moments of weakness, please remind me that I am coming home—and that the destination is well worth the journey.

PREPARE FOR SUDDEN SQUALLS

Lord, how those are increased who trouble me!
Many are those who rise up against me.
Psalm 3:1 SKJV

No matter what we like doing outdoors, we're wise to check the weather before we start.

Boaters need to beware of turbulent lakes or seas. Hikers should know when a possible downpour could create a flash flood. Mountain climbers must avoid those areas where violent winds and snowstorms could ruin their adventure.

But we don't have to be outdoors to encounter stormy weather. An argument at home, competition at work, a bully at school—all these "squalls" can blow up suddenly and create difficult, dangerous situations for us.

We can be thankful we have an escape. By prayer and the

indwelling power of God we can stay on an even keel in the most troubled waters and come through them unharmed.

Blessed are the peacemakers in the midst of the storm!

FOR FURTHER THOUGHT

When have you encountered "stormy weather" in your life? How did you find peace?

How does the story of Jesus in the storm (Mark 4:35–41) speak to your spirit?

PRAYER

Lord, I should probably expect trouble today. Please guard my mouth, strengthen my heart, and give me the humble spirit of Jesus.

AN EVER-HELPFUL SIDEKICK

Yes, though I walk through the valley of the shadow of death, I will not fear evil, for You are with me. Your rod and Your staff, they comfort me.

PSALM 23:4 SKJV

The lowly hiking staff is a versatile implement of a thousand-and-one uses. Well, at least seventy-eight.

It functions as a sturdy "third leg," helping us maintain stability when maneuvering over uneven terrain. It slows our momentum when the path leads downward and helps push us forward when the trail ascends. We can use the staff to probe surrounding vegetation for unpleasant surprises or to test soft ground too dangerous to walk on. With only a little ingenuity we could create an emergency fishing rod from it.

Like the hiking staff, there's another trusty helper at our

side as we travel through life. Our God is ever present to help us past every obstacle—emotional, mental, or spiritual. His power will get us up the mountains and carry us through the dark valleys of trouble and strife. His wisdom is always on call for moments both mundane and challenging.

Don't go anywhere without Him!

FOR FURTHER THOUGHT

What kind of "walking sticks" have you leaned on in life? Why?

When have you passed through a dark valley? What did the Lord do to help?

PRAYER

Lord, thank You for the reminder that You are with me always.

PROPERLY DRESSED

Therefore, as God's chosen people, holy and dearly loved, clothe yourselves with compassion, kindness, humility, gentleness and patience.
COLOSSIANS 3:12 NIV

There's a certain science to dressing for a cool- or cold-weather adventure.

"Layering" is designed to balance temperature and moisture levels both inside and out. The inner or base layer, often a polyester item, is supposed to draw sweat away from the skin. The middle or insulating layer, typically wool or fleece, keeps the body warm. The outer or shell layer keeps the worst of the wind and rain away from the other clothing. Together, each layer contributes to the wearer's comfort and protection.

The Bible often likens our Christian preparation to a wardrobe—whether the "armor of God" as described in Ephesians 6:10–18 or the "adornment. . .of a gentle and quiet spirit" mentioned in 1 Peter 3:3–4 (NIV). In Colossians 3, the apostle Paul suggested the layering of such spiritual clothes as compassion, kindness, humility, gentleness, and patience.

If we're dressed like that, we'll be safe and comfortable no matter what storms blow around us.

FOR FURTHER THOUGHT

Have you ever been caught in a storm without proper clothing? What was that like?

Can you recall a time when you needed the armor of God? How did that turn out?

PRAYER

Lord God, may I dress my spirit as carefully as I do my physical body.

ENJOYING GOD'S LOVE

"The Lord your God is with you, the Mighty Warrior who saves. He will take great delight in you; in his love he will no longer rebuke you, but will rejoice over you with singing."
ZEPHANIAH 3:17 NIV

Here's something to consider: naturally beautiful places—rivers, lakes, mountains, beaches—are yet another demonstration of God's love.

One avid fly fisherman put it this way: "One day when I was out on the river, it was as if I heard the voice of God telling me that He put that river there *for me,* that He created the fish I was trying to catch *for me*. . .that He was there *for me.* For the first time in my life—standing waist deep in that river—I came to know God as a loving Father who truly enjoys spending time with me while I am doing one of the things I love most."

Enjoy the beauty of God's creation when you spend a day at your favorite stream. Enjoy the natural beauty, the peace and solitude, and the fish. But remember, your heavenly Father is there, enjoying those things *with you*!

FOR FURTHER THOUGHT

Do you ever doubt that God loves you? Why or why not?

How can you know beyond a shadow of a doubt that He loves you deeply?

PRAYER

Father God, remind me that the beauty I enjoy when I'm streamside is Your special gift for me to enjoy—simply because You love me!

JUST KEEP GOING

Blessed is the one who perseveres under trial because, having stood the test, that person will receive the crown of life that the Lord has promised to those who love him.

JAMES 1:12 NIV

Hikers often find that the first half hour of any walk is the hardest. That's when most trekkers drop out. But the experienced hiker knows better times are ahead. After those initial aches and pains, a new energy arises. The body steps up a gear, allowing comfortable walking for much of the day. Beginners who persevere find themselves completing routes they wouldn't have contemplated before.

The walk of faith is not the easy stroll some expect it to be. In fact, it can be rockier than many mountain trails—and some people give up before they really get started.

But eventually the wind will be at your back—a new, God-given energy will propel you along the path. You'll do things for Him you could never have imagined at the beginning of your walk—if you just keep going.

FOR FURTHER THOUGHT

What were your expectations when you first started your journey with the Lord? How did they compare with the reality?

How well do you persevere under trial? How can you grow in this area?

PRAYER

Dear Lord, You made us capable of great things—please convince me of that! Through Your work I am better than I ever realized I could be.

DANIEL BOONE'S RELIGION

"You shall love the Lord your God. . .
and. . .love your neighbor as yourself."
MATTHEW 22:37, 39 SKJV

On Sundays, young Daniel Boone walked with his mother to the Quaker meetinghouse, carrying an old English gun for protection against Indians and wild animals. On the gun's butt was carved "D. Boon. 1746. my Mother Chirch Gun."

Daniel Boone grew up on a frontier farm in Pennsylvania. From his father he learned to hunt, farm, tan leather, use carpenter's tools, and work a blacksmith's forge. From his mother he inherited the religious convictions that stayed with him all his long life.

A restless pioneer, Daniel walked westward with his family, blazing a trail called the Wilderness Road, building the first fort (Boonesborough) on the Kentucky River, and mapping routes through the wilds of North Carolina, Tennessee, and Virginia. At the age of eighty-two, he was seen hunting alone in Nebraska.

As an old man, in a letter to his sister-in-law, Daniel Boone expressed his faith and life's code: "I am as ignorant as a Child. All the Religion I have is to Love and fear God, believe in Jesus Christ, Do all the good to my Neighbors and my Self that I can. . .and trust in God's mercy for the Rest."

FOR FURTHER THOUGHT

Growing up, what did you learn about faith from your parents or guardians? Was it positive or negative?

Who or what has had the greatest impact on your Christian walk?

PRAYER

Thank You, Father, for the simplicity of "true religion."

JOY IN THE ACCOMPLISHMENT

All Judah rejoiced concerning the oath,
for they had sworn with all their heart and
had sought Him earnestly, and He let them find
Him. So the LORD gave them rest on every side.

2 CHRONICLES 15:15 NASB

There's a special feeling of accomplishment we get when we reach the end of a difficult trail or the peak of the mountain. We experience the full satisfaction of having met our goals.

Having pursued our destination to the end—without breaking a leg or breaking up our marriage—we can relax and drink in the outdoor splendor. Rest feels good when all our hard work has paid off.

God also gives a wonderful rest when we've sought Him with our whole heart. The children of Judah had entered into a covenant to seek God, making a commitment to put Him first. It took work on their part, but they rejoiced greatly when they reached their goal.

On our own difficult journeys, we can feel God strengthening us when we don't give up. When we reach the point of rest, let's experience the joy of giving ourselves back to Him.

FOR FURTHER THOUGHT

When have you searched for God with your whole heart? What was that like?

When have you experienced the full rest of God? What was it like?

PRAYER

Lord, You've been so good to me.
I want to follow You wherever You go.

HIDDEN PARADISE

It is the glory of God to conceal a matter,
but the glory of kings is to search out a matter.
PROVERBS 25:2 NASB

Seeking adventure, a teenager followed the creek through the valley rather than the well-worn trail along the curved ridge. A century and a half earlier, a coal-hauling gravity railroad had run that ridge without a locomotive, descending on its own momentum, hauled up steep grades by metal cables and a stationary steam engine.

Little remained of that bygone era—only some rotted ties, tangled loops of ancient cable, an occasional rusted rail spike. And a tunnel, big enough to walk into, the creek running through it. Wide steps of flat stone lay dark and damp on the tunnel floor. High walls of stone supported massive slabs laid across the top, forming an aqueduct beneath the trail where the train once ran. Downstream, water cascaded into a small grotto surrounded by tall trees. Remarkable and haunting, this bit of history clothed in nature's camouflage. The boy named it Hidden Paradise.

He was fifteen then. Now fifty-five, he lives two hundred miles away but occasionally drives the distance for the hike. As he walks with his children's children to Hidden Paradise, new memories are laid up for the generations to come.

FOR FURTHER THOUGHT

What hidden treasures have you found in outdoor adventures? How do you share them?

What hidden treasures have you found in your faith walk? How do you share them?

PRAYER

Father, may I find what You have hidden—
and share those things with others around me.

INTO THE DARK

And God saw the light, that it was good,
and God divided the light from the darkness.
GENESIS 1:4 SKJV

Snorkeling off an atoll can be a beautiful and relaxing experience—on the inside of the reef. That's where the water is shallow, the visibility good, and the multicolored fish seemingly unconcerned by your presence.

But venture through a gap in the reef and everything changes. The currents are stronger, the water colder, and the marine life more menacing. Often the seabed disappears into an inky abyss. It can be a fascinating and enticing world—but venture in without a guide and you're taking a big risk.

Our whole world is like that. From above, where

Christians should be, some of those "lower things" can seem awfully enticing. But when we really look, we see they're dark and dangerous.

In this life, we won't always have a protective coral reef surrounding us. But if we have to venture outside, let's take the Lord Jesus as our guide.

FOR FURTHER THOUGHT

What makes unknown things so inviting? When have you found trouble pursuing them?

How can you protect yourself against dangers in the spiritual realm?

PRAYER

Jesus, Savior, I am often attracted to those lower things of life. Remind me today that what truly matters is within the warmth of Your love.

THE NEED TO TURN AROUND

But those who want to get rich fall into temptation and a trap, and many foolish and harmful desires which plunge people into ruin and destruction. . . . But flee from these things, you man of God, and pursue righteousness, godliness, faith, love, perseverance, and gentleness.

1 TIMOTHY 6:9, 11 NASB

Along the brushy edges of fields, foxes are first-class hunters. Using their eyes, ears, and noses, they are alert to everything that moves, makes a sound, or gives off a scent. They present an image of graceful control as they travel at an easy trot in search of dinner.

Foxes are wise in the ways of their world—but a hunter can fool them by imitating the sound of a small animal in trouble. It's a rare fox that will not abandon its plans and come on the run for the free meal it thinks is waiting.

That's when a fox is vulnerable. But let him get one glimpse of the hunter and he'll forget all about that free meal. He'll reverse course without a second thought and sprint away to put as much distance as possible between himself and danger. The fox doesn't hesitate, thinking how good a rabbit dinner would be. He just runs.

We do well to make a similar retreat as soon as we recognize spiritual danger.

FOR FURTHER THOUGHT

Do you remember a time when you almost fell to temptation? How did you escape?

Have there been times when you did give in to temptation? How did that turn out?

PRAYER

Lord, help me to remember Your precepts and flee temptation as soon as I recognize it.

WHAT ARE YOU FISHING FOR?

He said to them, "Go into all the world and preach the gospel to all creation."
MARK 16:15 NIV

Have you ever thought of your outdoor adventures as a setting for service? As a place to honor the God who made you one of His very own?

"Come, follow me"—Jesus called out to Andrew and his brother, Peter, the fisherman turned apostle who would one day take a place of prominence in the Lord's church—"and I will send you out to fish for people" (Mark 1:17 NIV). God may not call us to leave everything for full-time service, the way He did Peter. But He has commanded every one of us to "preach the gospel" in the places He puts us.

Guys with a passion for fly-fishing know their fellow

anglers are a friendly sort, the kind of people who enjoy discussing the day they're having streamside. So when you set out on your fishing trip—or any other outdoor adventure—make sure you take with you the message of God's love and salvation. Your fellow adventurers might be ready to hear and accept that truth.

FOR FURTHER THOUGHT

Have you ever spoken up—or kept quiet—about the gospel with a fellow adventurer? How did that go?

What makes it easy to share Jesus with your outdoor buddies? What makes that difficult?

PRAYER

My Savior, remind me daily that You can use everything You give me—including my time in the outdoors—as a tool to reach others for You.

A SKILLFUL HUNTER

Esau was a skillful hunter, a man of the field, and Jacob was a plain man, dwelling in tents.
GENESIS 25:27 SKJV

Esau is the most famous hunter in the Bible. While his twin brother, Jacob, was content to stay close to home, overseeing the camp, Esau loved to roam the wild country. He lived for the thrill of the chase. He was probably supposed to be overseeing the herdsmen, but he was the boss' son and the herds were fine. . .so what was to stop him from the occasional hunting trip? Scripture identifies Esau as "a skillful hunter."

He was set to inherit the bulk of his father's vast flocks and herds, but he traded it all away for one bowl of stew. Esau's priorities were completely out of whack. Unfortunately, he was out perfecting his hunting skills when maybe he should have been shepherding.

Esau would have made a top "big game guide." He could have taught us all a thing or two about tracking and hunting. But when it comes to priorities—putting a value on the family business and keeping the camp going—that's where we have to look to Jacob.

FOR FURTHER THOUGHT

How important to you are your hobbies? How much time do you spend with them in comparison to more important things?

How would you rank the top priorities in your life? What adjustments might that list need?

PRAYER

God, please help me to keep my passion for the outdoors in the proper perspective.

SEEING HUMOR IN THE OUTDOORS

A merry heart does good like a medicine.

PROVERBS 17:22 SKJV

Sometimes during our time in the outdoors, we can open our eyes and ears to observe what's going on around us. . .and burst into laughter.

It's not difficult to find humor in the natural world. The overprotective blackbird scolding you and buzzing around your head as it defends its nest against a perceived threat. . .the beaver that lifts its head out of the water, sending you a bucktoothed grin. . .the river otters playfully seeking a creative angle of attack on their mates. And who can't see the humor in being kept awake on an overnight camping trip by a romantic male bullfrog calling out to the opposite sex?

God created everything we see in the outdoors, and He allows us to enjoy it all. He also created humor—and if we pay close enough attention, we might just find a good laugh in the world of nature. When you do, think of God smiling and laughing with you at some of nature's most humorous sights and sounds.

FOR FURTHER THOUGHT

Have you ever found humor in something in nature? What made it so funny?

How does humor fit into God's personality?

PRAYER

Father, thank You for allowing me to see the lightness and humor You've strategically placed throughout creation—just for Your children to enjoy!

A MINDFUL CREATOR

When I consider your heavens, the work of your fingers, the moon and the stars, which you have set in place, what is mankind that you are mindful of them, human beings that you care for them?

PSALM 8:3–4 NIV

One of the best parts of camping is sitting out in the fresh air, just looking up and enjoying the beauty of the night sky. Away from city lights, you can see more stars than some people know exist—and if you're out at the right time of year, you can try counting the "shooting stars" during the Perseid meteor shower, an annual display of celestial fireworks that people have been watching since at least the time of Christ.

Even more wondrous than the night sky, however, is

contemplating the love of the God who made it all.

It's difficult to fully comprehend how the God who simply spoke our cosmos into existence could have the time or the inclination to think about us. But He does—and for that reason we can enjoy both the wonders of creation and the love of our Creator.

FOR FURTHER THOUGHT

How does God show His love for you in nature?

What elements of nature remind you the most of God? Why?

PRAYER

My Father and Creator, I can't begin to express my joy, gratitude, and amazement that You made such an awesome universe. . .yet Your thoughts are on me!

GREATER THAN OUR DISABILITY

So Mephibosheth lived in Jerusalem,
because he ate at the king's table regularly.
And he was disabled in his two feet.
2 SAMUEL 9:13 NASB

Can a wheelchair-bound person enjoy the outdoors like those with full use of their limbs? More and more, the answer is yes.

Inventors with a heart for the disabled have created "wheelchairs" with motorized tank tracks; heavy-duty, four-wheeled, people-powered chairs; and snow skis fitted with seats, among other things. Physical disability shouldn't keep anyone from experiencing the outdoors.

Neither should our spiritual disabilities keep us from enjoying God. With our prominent character flaws and self-esteem issues, we may sometimes think that closeness to God is impossible. But He "invents" ways of bridging that gap, treating us as King David did the crippled grandson of his predecessor, King Saul. Mephibosheth had done nothing for David—it was only the king's kindness that brought the young man to the royal table.

Our King has invited us to dine with Him. God's kindness is greater than our disabilities.

FOR FURTHER THOUGHT

What are your "disabilities" that would keep you from dining with the Lord? How has He overcome them?

How can you encourage someone with physical disabilities to enjoy the outdoors?

PRAYER

*Lord, thank You that You invite me—
with all my disabilities—to Your table.*

CALLING OUT BOLDLY

Therefore let's approach the throne of grace with confidence, so that we may receive mercy and find grace for help at the time of our need.

HEBREWS 4:16 NASB

The exploration of caves is called spelunking. (Some have defined the term *spelunk* as "the sound of a forehead hitting a stalactite after running in terror in pitch blackness.")

Wandering about in cold, damp darkness isn't everyone's idea of fun, but it can be instructive for all of us. For example, if you've made a bad turn in a cave and can't find your way back, disregard the impulse to move and simply stay put. Shout every couple of minutes to help your partner or a rescue party locate you (and probably carry you out to treat that ugly bruise on your forehead).

It's not only in the blackness of a cave that we lose our bearings. Life can be dark, confusing, and frightening at times, but God's advice is like that of the spelunking corps: resist the impulse to run. Instead, simply rest where you are and call out to Him. God's ears are always open, and He's always ready to rescue.

FOR FURTHER THOUGHT

Do you think you would enjoy spelunking? Why or why not?

Have you ever lost your bearings in the darkness, either physical or spiritual? What did you do to find your way into the light?

PRAYER

Lord, may I draw near to You today,
calling out boldly for Your help.

SHARK CAGE

"Be strong and of good courage. Do not be afraid or be dismayed, for the LORD your God is with you wherever you go."
JOSHUA 1:9 SKJV

If you ever have the privilege of visiting Australia's Great Barrier Reef, you'll see that it's full of examples of God's creation.

Shark encounters are common in the reef, usually with gray nurse sharks that pose no threat to swimmers. Since they're well fed from the abundance of fish in the area, they pay little attention to humans. For more adventure, though, you can go farther out into the ocean where the great white sharks concentrate. But you'll want to be in a shark cage.

From the safety of the cage, you can see these magnificent

creatures up close—and realize just how fearsome they are. Your safety depends on those metal bars surrounding you—without them, you'd be in trouble.

We live in a world full of trouble, and there are plenty of "sharks" just waiting to attack and eat us alive. In God's presence, though, we can know that we'll always be protected from harm.

FOR FURTHER THOUGHT

What kind of "cage" do you need for protection in the world today?

How does God's presence protect you from the dangers of this world?

PRAYER

Lord, thank You for watching over me and protecting me from the predators of this world.

THE IMPORTANCE OF STRENGTH

"Do not grieve, for the joy of the Lord is your strength."

NEHEMIAH 8:10 NIV

What fisherman hasn't hooked into the really big one—then wondered if his line and knots would hold strong against that fish struggling for freedom?

Anglers understand the importance of using equipment strong enough for the size and type of fish they're after. They also recognize that their equipment is only as strong as the knots they use to attach their lures to their line.

There's a similar principle in our daily walk with Jesus. It's important to equip ourselves with strong faith, a firm grasp of scripture, and a consistent, abiding prayer life. But unless we tie all those things together with the simple joy of knowing and serving God, they won't hold firm when tests come our way.

Consider the source of your strength. The power you need to live the Christian life depends on your allowing the "knot" of God's joy to dwell strongly and consistently within you.

FOR FURTHER THOUGHT

What do you do to secure the "knot" of your relationship with God?

Have you ever sensed the knot slipping? What can you do to restore its strength?

PRAYER

Lord, help me to remember that my walk with You is only as strong as the inner joy I allow You to place within me.

THE BOOK OF MARVELS

"The grass withers and the flowers fall,
but the word of our God endures forever."
ISAIAH 40:8 NIV

A few generations back, one author captured childhood imaginations like few others: Richard Halliburton, a 1930s adventurer who flew from one nerve-racking exploit to the next in a biplane named *The Flying Carpet.*

Among Halliburton's exploits were a swim through the Panama Canal (for a fee of thirty-six cents) and spending the night alone with a mummified pharaoh in a tomb of the Great Pyramid of Giza. Halliburton was a personal friend of Lawrence of Arabia and fraternized with the French Foreign Legion in Timbuktu. In eighteen months, Halliburton circumnavigated the globe, logging nearly thirty-four thousand miles and visiting thirty-four countries.

On March 3, 1939, Halliburton undertook a new adventure—to sail a Chinese junk across the Pacific Ocean to San Francisco. But later that month, communication with Halliburton stopped. He was declared dead October 5, 1939.

The adventurer once bragged, "There is no book of marvels like my Books of Marvels." But he was wrong. There are sixty-six marvelous books of wonder and truth in God's Book, the Holy Bible.

FOR FURTHER THOUGHT

How important is God's Book to you? How much time do you spend in its pages?

How can you demonstrate the Bible's value to others?

PRAYER

When I read Your Word, Father, bring fresh wonder to my heart; let me find refreshment for my day.

DON'T FORGET TO LOOK UP

He determines the number of the stars
and calls them each by name.
PSALM 147:4 NIV

When we're out fishing, hunting, hiking—whatever we like to do outside—it's easy to become so focused on our particular activity that we forget to look around us and see the amazing reflection of God in His creation.

Not only has God created all the things you see and put them in place, He also has each one numbered and named. And still He cares for *you*! When King David looked out at the vast majesty of creation, he was moved to ask, "What is mankind that you are mindful of them, human beings that you care for them?" (Psalm 8:4 NIV).

When you're enjoying your favorite activities, don't forget

to look up. Get a glimpse of the greatness, the creativity, and the splendor of God. Then consider the fact that this very same God thinks about you daily, loves you deeply, and provides for you generously.

FOR FURTHER THOUGHT

When was the last time you were outside and really saw the beauty of creation? When can you go next?

How might you see God's care for you in creation?

PRAYER

Father God, help me to see all of creation as a reflection of who You really are and what You can really do.

WHAT KIND OF SOIL ARE YOU?

He spoke many things to them in parables,
saying, "Behold, a sower went forth to sow."
MATTHEW 13:3 SKJV

In the cool of a brilliant spring morning, a man went out to tend his recently planted garden. He drank in the sweet, earthy smell of the soil and noticed some seeds beginning to sprout. A few leaped up out of the soil. Others were just breaking into the light. Weeds were already trying to choke some others. Remembering the parable of the soils, the man thought of his own heart, asking, *Which one of these am I?*

In certain seasons of our lives, we resemble the seed sown on the side of the road. We're consumed by the cares of this world, without time for God. Sometimes we feel a strong surge in our faith, only to quickly run dry like the seed sown on shallow, rocky ground. Yet other times, we're surrounded by the "thorns" of people or attitudes that choke our faith.

Today it's worth examining ourselves to know which of Jesus' soils best describes us. Dig deep—and make whatever changes are necessary to your mental, emotional, and spiritual health.

FOR FURTHER THOUGHT

What type of soil best describes you? Why?

What can you do to encourage spiritual growth in your heart?

PRAYER

Lord, please tend the soil of my heart, making me productive for You.

STAY WITH IT

Let us not be weary in doing good, for in due season we shall reap, if we do not faint.
GALATIANS 6:9 SKJV

Hikers, bikers, and swimmers do well to remember this commonsense idea: going out is always easier than coming back.

While you might feel fine on the first leg of the journey, the doubling back may leave you weary, blistered, and cramped—possibly even in danger. But if you travel too far on the way out, you can't just quit—especially if you're swimming. Somehow, you've got to find the reserves to keep moving, heading for home, like the hummingbird that flies, nonstop, over the Gulf of Mexico on its annual migration.

There's a parallel here to the Christian life. The apostle

Paul encouraged us to "not be weary in doing good," to keep moving forward whatever the difficulties. We might be tired when we're done, but there is a reward—the "reaping" we enjoy "in due season."

So don't faint. Stay with it!

FOR FURTHER THOUGHT

Can you think of a time when you were tempted to give up? What happened?

How did you feel about the choice you made, whether to quit or continue?

PRAYER

Lord, I get tired on this journey. Help me to "not be weary in doing good" and never faint along the way.

TWO KINDS OF CLIMBING

Look! The wages you failed to pay the workers who mowed your fields are crying out against you.

James 5:4 NIV

Many measure their lives based on profit, victory, and achievement. Others gauge themselves by the lives they touch, the joys they share, and the people they help along the way.

Climbing—whether a mountain or the corporate ladder—can be exhausting. At the end of a business day, the weariness is both physical and emotional. Fighting corporate wars can leave us scarred and empty, without comfort in our old age.

Climbing a mountain is tiring too, although that toll can be overcome by a nourishing meal, laughter with friends, and a good night's rest. The natural high and sense of accomplishment last for years.

Jesus Christ wants to free us from the treadmill of worldly achievement and replace it with a walk in high places—one that fills the emptiness and soothes the wounds. He's waiting for us to take Him up on His offer.

FOR FURTHER THOUGHT

How have you typically measured your life? How does that align with the Lord's plan and purpose for you?

What changes might you want to make to bring more value to life—your own and others'?

PRAYER

Dear God, free me from the wars of life and put me on Your mountain path. May I be bold, excited, and all out for You today.

ALWAYS BE PREPARED

Always be prepared to give an answer to everyone who asks you to give the reason for the hope that you have.

1 PETER 3:15 NIV

No matter what your outdoor activity of choice—camping, hiking, fishing, biking—it's vital that you go into that activity prepared for anything that could come your way. Failure here can dampen your enjoyment and sometimes even lead to danger. Outdoor life is filled with the unexpected, which is why we need to prepare ourselves for anything and everything.

That's as true in the workaday world—where you make your living, go to church, and care for your family and friends—as it is in the outdoor realm. Preparation is also key when it comes to using your love of the outdoors as a vehicle for sharing your faith.

Few things in life help form friendships like sharing in outdoor adventures. So when you're at the lake, or on the river, or climbing a mountain, or hiking or biking that amazing trail, be prepared—because the person you're with might need to hear what's most important to you: not the creation but the Creator, the amazing, hope-inspiring, loving God you serve.

FOR FURTHER THOUGHT

Why might the outdoors provide a strong opportunity for Christian witness?

When have you been able to share your faith with a fellow adventurer? How did that go?

PRAYER

Remind me daily, my gracious heavenly Father, to be prepared for whatever and whoever You send my way.

SONG OF THE STARS

Praise him, sun and moon; praise him,
all you shining stars.
Psalm 148:3 NIV

When is the last time you stood alone in the night, watching the stars?

God's handiwork can be millions of miles away—yet as close as a quiet moment in the backyard. Did you ever stop to think that you are seeing the same stars that shone on King David, Christopher Columbus, and George Washington? Those stars were placed on the day God created the heavens, and they still point us to our powerful Lord today.

So many of us are caught up in the rat race, searching for peace but missing some of the quiet signposts to God's presence. The night sky holds a million secrets—and waits for us to step away from this hectic world and reach for His hand.

If your life seems to be careening out of control, stop the treadmill. Pull the power cord of your existence for a while, and listen to the song of the stars. Your Creator waits on you tonight.

FOR FURTHER THOUGHT

When and where have you seen the stars at their clearest? How did that affect you?

What does the vastness of space tell you about God?

PRAYER

Gracious God, my Creator, please help me to stop racing long enough to hear Your voice when I gaze in wonder at the stars.

REST IN THE LORD

Some trust in chariots and some in horses,
but we trust in the name of the Lord our God.
Psalm 20:7 NIV

An old pastor, a World War II veteran, had survived a kamikaze attack on his destroyer. The explosion on board threw him into the Pacific Ocean. He was in one piece, but the thought of being in the water unnerved him. Not a Christian at the time, prayer was unfamiliar. He struggled and fought the waves for some time.

After a while, though, his training came to mind. He remembered he was wearing a flotation jacket and realized his struggling was in vain. It would only exhaust him, make him weak, and likely lead to his death. But if he relaxed and let the jacket hold him up, he had a better chance of rescue.

The vest could do for him what he couldn't do for himself.

Later, after he became a Christian, the man shared this story with others going through rough times. We can fight in our own strength and wear ourselves out. . .or we can relax in the Lord, letting Him keep us afloat until He brings us through.

FOR FURTHER THOUGHT

How does being a Christian help you when you experience rough times?

What helps you trust the Lord instead of your own or others' strength?

PRAYER

Lord, teach me to rest in You and not to struggle against my circumstances.

AFTER THE SUMMIT

Then you shall walk in your way safely,
and your foot shall not stumble.
PROVERBS 3:23 SKJV

That moment when you reach the peak of a mountain is like the moment you finally "get" God. It's wonderful, but your work isn't done. Having climbed that mountain, many an inexperienced hiker thinks it will be easier on the way down. That's often when maps are neglected and steps get careless. But more hikers become lost or injured on the way down from a summit than on the way up.

Life can be like that. When you come to faith, despite what you might expect, things aren't all sunshine and roses. Oh, life will be good, and things will make much more sense—but you still need to watch your footing and check your direction.

Too much bother? In the elation of conquering a mountain or finding God, it can sometimes seem so. But paying attention and walking with care will see you safely home in both instances.

FOR FURTHER THOUGHT

When you trusted your life to Christ, how did you expect your life to go? What was your actual experience?

When have you gotten careless in your Christian life? How did you get back on track?

PRAYER

Lord Jesus, finding You seems like the ultimate achievement. . .but following in Your footsteps will be the crowning glory of my life.

JOIN THE RESCUE TEAM

You were as sheep going astray but are now returned to the Shepherd and Bishop of your souls.

1 PETER 2:25 SKJV

When someone gets in trouble at higher elevations, a mountain rescue team is usually nearby, ready to lend a hand. Members of these teams are usually climbers themselves and almost always volunteers. Each time they go out to bring an injured climber or lost hiker back, they put themselves in danger.

Why?

The most common answer is that they hope someone would do the same for them. That's probably true, but there's something about the hard realities of the thin air that reminds folks we are all in this together.

With that in mind, let's consider our own fellow travelers: some are on the right path, others are hurt, others are straying into danger. Step up and volunteer for heaven's rescue team, and do your part to bring them all home safely.

FOR FURTHER THOUGHT

When have you helped someone get back on the right path, either physically or spiritually? What was that like?

When has another person rescued you from straying? How did you feel about that?

PRAYER

Lord, I know You'll rejoice in my safe arrival in heaven. Please give me the wisdom and courage to help guide others into your loving, eternal presence.

STRONGER TOGETHER

So Peter was kept in prison, but the church was earnestly praying to God for him.
ACTS 12:5 NIV

Kayak instructors sometimes play a little game with learning paddlers: they "raft up."

Calling all the kayaks alongside each other, they tell the boaters to lay their paddles across their bows. As each person grips their own paddle and that of a neighbor, there's enough stability for someone to walk or crawl along the backs of all the kayaks then make their way around the fronts.

Normally, it's just a simple exercise for beginners—but if that group were to be caught in a storm, "rafting up" would provide stability and security for everyone. It might even save a life.

Church is a lot like that. In our modern society, church can take second place to a comfortable bed, household chores, or sporting events on any given Sunday. But in times of personal need or persecution, "rafting up" with fellow believers can make all the difference.

Will you be in church this Sunday?

FOR FURTHER THOUGHT

How would you rate your church connection currently? How could it be better?

When have you seen believers pulling together in positive ways? What does that say to other people?

PRAYER

Father, thank You for Your support system here on earth. Help me to remember that even if I don't need the help right now, I can provide some for a brother or a sister in Christ.

A FRESH BURST OF ENERGY

So we built the wall, and the entire wall was joined together to half its height, for the people had a mind to work.

NEHEMIAH 4:6 NASB

It's amazing what we can accomplish when we set our minds to it. But we have to resist the urge to quit when we get tired or frustrated along the way.

Think about your experience in the outdoors. We've all been tempted to turn back at the first cramp in our side or pain in the shin. But seeing the trail marker near the end of the journey brings cheer to our heart. Glimpsing the peak gives us a spurt of energy that propels us to the top.

Our spiritual life is a long journey, filled with difficulties and reverses. But when we sense that we've reached a milestone of some sort, it's as if God is encouraging us:

"You can make this happen! This is doable!"

Today let's be like Nehemiah and his people, with "a mind to work." Between us and God, we can accomplish amazing things.

FOR FURTHER THOUGHT

What kind of encouragement do you need right now to trust God? Who do you know who provides that kind of encouragement?

What role does prayer play in the achieving of goals? How would you rate your prayer life?

PRAYER

Lord, encourage me to continue on my path—
and please keep working in my life!

THE ROCKS CRY OUT

Let everything that has breath praise the Lord. Praise the Lord.
Psalm 150:6 NIV

As Jesus rode into Jerusalem, His followers began cheering Him. The Pharisees, grumpy as always, told Jesus to silence the crowd. But Jesus answered that if the people stopped praising Him, the very rocks would cry out.

Imagine that! Everything that exists in nature—trees, grass, rivers and seas, clouds, mountains, even the rocks underfoot—testify to God's majesty.

If you look at the rocks around you, you'll notice that they're composed of a variety of minerals. Certain kinds are harder than others. Some are huge boulders; others are tiny bits of gravel. There are white rocks, brown rocks, gray rocks, multicolored rocks.

Those rocks are a picture of humanity. There are many sizes, shapes, styles, and colors of people. But we all have the ability to recognize that our Creator is worthy of praise.

So what are you waiting for?

FOR FURTHER THOUGHT

How often do you stop to notice rocks, leaves, animals, and other aspects of nature? What do they tell you about God?

How quick are you to offer praise to God? Why?

PRAYER

Lord, I thank You for the constant reminders all around me that You are the God of all creation.

THE NEXT DAY'S JOURNEY

"You are already clean because of the word which I have spoken to you."

JOHN 15:3 NASB

High up in a horse's saddle, things are different. We see a different perspective of our surroundings. We travel a greater distance than we would on foot.

After a long day on the trail, though, the animal will need care and grooming. We'll offer it hay and water. We'll clear its tail of ticks and tangles. We'll scour its hooves for mud and manure.

There are parallels here to our own spiritual journey. God has given us His saddle-height view of the world, helping us to see life from a loftier perspective. At His direction we've traveled further down the road of transformation than we ever expected to. Through His Word we can be filled and cleansed.

The Bible restores our faith, purifies our minds, and strengthens our resolve. Without it, we won't be ready for the next day's journey.

FOR FURTHER THOUGHT

Do you view the future with optimism or pessimism? Why?

How would you rate the quality of your personal Bible study? How could you improve it?

PRAYER

Lord Jesus, please speak to me through Your Word—I need Your strength for the next day's journey.

LIVING ON THE EDGE

By faith he made his home in the promised land like a stranger in a foreign country; he lived in tents, as did Isaac and Jacob, who were heirs with him of the same promise.

HEBREWS 11:9 NIV

Most outdoors people get a rush out of tent life in nature. Long fishing trips or family campouts have their difficulties and inconveniences, but they can be exhilarating.

It's a different story when you live in a tent full-time like Abraham, Isaac, and Jacob did. They dwelled in Beersheba and Beer Lahai Roi in the Negev, the arid south of Canaan. As Isaiah 30:6 (NIV) says, the Negev was "a land of hardship and distress, of lions and lionesses, of adders and darting snakes."

What drove these men to pitch their tents there? Well,

they needed a toehold in Canaan, and they believed God's promise—that He would give them the entire land—so they were willing to make their home in a region of "hardship and distress." That's faith.

The next time you feel like giving up, remember the patriarchs, living on the edge, pounding their tent pegs into the Promised Land.

FOR FURTHER THOUGHT

When you feel overwhelmed by life, where do you go for peace?

In what situations have you had only God's promises to cling to? How did things work out?

PRAYER

God, give me the faith that if I simply believe, holding on to Your promises, You'll come through for me.

ARROWHEADS

Do not be conformed to this world,
but be transformed by the renewing of your mind.
ROMANS 12:2 NASB

Long before gun and archery shops, men had to make their own tools for hunting.

Arrowheads, spearheads, and knives were "knapped" from various stones. A skilled knapper could take raw material and hammer away bits and flakes with another stone, creating a sharp, finished point that was attached to an arrow or a spear for hunting. Primitive men armed with stone-tipped spears could bring down large, dangerous animals, which were used for food and clothing.

God "knaps" us in much the same way. He takes us, lumps of rough, raw material, and lovingly works us, bit by bit and flake by flake, into a perfect tool He can use for His purposes.

Through our many life experiences, we can be knapped for His perfect ways—if only we'll allow Him to perform His work.

FOR FURTHER THOUGHT

In what ways has God "knapped" you? What did you think of the process at the time?

How much progress has God made on you? How committed are you to allowing Him to finish the job?

PRAYER

Lord, I commit myself into Your hands today. Please shape me into whatever You want me to be.

A DIFFERENT KIND OF FISHING

"Come, follow me," Jesus said,
"and I will send you out to fish for people."
MATTHEW 4:19 NIV

Up north in Michigan and Minnesota, where real fishing experts pursue real fish (that would be walleye and northern pike), anglers take their sport seriously. A note on a bait shop bulletin board explains it best: "If I'm not back by sundown, tell my bride-to-be and the preacher to express regrets—the walleye are biting!"

Jesus' appeal for anglers was for a different kind of fishing, of course. To men who knew what fishing was all about, continuing their trade with the Lord was an invitation they couldn't turn down. Recognizing they had been "caught" and changed by Jesus, it was now their turn to "fish."

Without the benefit of seminary or any ministry training, they dropped their nets and followed their new calling with an even greater passion than that with which they'd made a living. That way is open to us too.

FOR FURTHER THOUGHT

Why do you think Jesus used fishing to teach life lessons? How can you apply those lessons to your life today?

When is the last time you shared your faith? Who can you reach out to today with the message of salvation?

PRAYER

Jesus, give me the same enthusiasm for soul-winning that I have for my hobbies. Help me to influence my friends and family for You!

IN THE FULL LIGHT OF DAY

The path of the righteous is like the morning sun,
shining ever brighter till the full light of day.
PROVERBS 4:18 NIV

A couple was hiking and camping in a wilderness area. Rising early one morning, they packed up by lantern and hiked a length of trail by flashlight to a scenic overlook. Upon arriving, they dropped their packs and sat on a large rock, huddling together for warmth.

As the morning sun began to peek over the mountains, it slowly painted the valley below in blues and greens and the sky above in breathtaking reds and purples. But only when the sun was fully up and shining brightly could they see, far below them, the riverside trail they'd be taking that day.

That's a good picture of our lives. We spend a lot of time

living and working in the dark—or by the limited light of our own wisdom. It's only when we let the light of God's Word shine on our lives that we can see where our true path lies.

FOR FURTHER THOUGHT

Have you ever not known what God was calling you to do? What helped you find His path?

How have you found scripture to be a light for your path (Psalm 119:105)?

PRAYER

Creator God, help me to see the path You have set for me by the light of Your Word.

WALK IN THE LIGHT

But if we walk in the light, as he is in the light, we have fellowship with one another, and the blood of Jesus, his Son, purifies us from all sin.

1 JOHN 1:7 NIV

We campers can't get enough of our favorite activity. No matter how many times we've been "out there," it never gets old. There are so many things to experience and enjoy:

- Breathing the fresh, open air—exhilarating
- Sitting around a campfire with family and friends—uplifting
- Cooking freshly caught fish outdoors—delightful
- Lying in a sleeping bag under the moon and stars—awesome

- Listening to the symphony of nocturnal creatures—tranquil

But getting up in the wee hours, finding the flashlight dead, tripping over rocks, stubbing your toe on a tree root, or turning your ankle in a hole—that's no fun at all.

That's what life is like when we're separated from our true light, Jesus Christ. By all means, walk in the light!

FOR FURTHER THOUGHT

When have your outdoor activities been happy and fulfilling? When have they been disappointing or hard?

How has Jesus lit your way through life?

PRAYER

Lord, this world is so dark spiritually. Please help me always to walk in the light of Your Word so I won't stumble and fall.

APPLES AND. . .APPLES

"Every tree is known by its own fruit."
LUKE 6:44 SKJV

The sluggish swamp covered a couple of acres. There were small islands of spongy grass and a brush-choked peninsula that poked into the black backwater. At the end of the solid ground stood a tree that promised afternoon refreshment. Mark hadn't noticed it before—it was hidden amid the rushes and the reeds. But now he could see ripe red fruit even across the wide, brackish water. Apples! He couldn't wait to eat one.

He scrambled up a wooded hillside, climbed down into the wash, picked his way across wet tufts of thick reeds, and pushed through the undergrowth to where the tree stood.

But what a disappointment—they were dry and bitter

crab apples. Henry David Thoreau described such wild fruit as "sour enough to set a squirrel's teeth on edge and make a jay scream."

We often work hard—go out of our way even—for things that look good but don't pay off in the end. Good fruit is a matter not of what the eye sees but of the nature of the plant. In our lives, if we are branches of God's fruitful vine, Jesus, we won't just "look good"—we'll bear fruit that feeds and refreshes many (see John 15:5–8).

FOR FURTHER THOUGHT

When have you sought after something that looked good but turned out not to be? What lessons did you learn?

What kind of "fruit" are you bearing right now? How can you ensure it's sweet and good?

PRAYER

Lord, You are the vine; I am a branch. Keep me closely connected to You so I can bear good fruit.

CHOOSING YOUR BATTLES

A prudent person sees evil and hides himself;
but the naive proceed, and pay the penalty.
PROVERBS 27:12 NASB

It would be a naive hiker indeed who, seeing a bear cub near the trail, would not stop in his tracks. Coming between a cub and its mother is an invitation to be attacked tooth and claw—the attraction of that "cute baby bear" is not worth risking the consequences.

Experienced observers know that getting too close to the young of many animals will bring a vigorous response from the mothers. In the case of certain birds, as with the grouse hen, the mother will flee from her chicks, acting as if she's unable to fly, in hopes of luring pursuers after her. When she's drawn a potential predator far enough away, she'll end the charade and take wing to save herself.

A prudent hiker sees a bear and gets out of the way. A prudent grouse sees danger and runs the other way. A prudent Christian sees evil and hides.

Let's not be naive and "pay the penalty."

FOR FURTHER THOUGHT

When have you faced an outdoors situation that might have hurt you or others? What did you do?

When have you faced a dangerous spiritual circumstance? What did you do?

PRAYER

Father God, please give me wisdom to avoid things that would harm me or others—to know Your paths and follow them.

OPEN OUR EYES

"As the heavens are higher than the earth,
so are My ways higher than your ways and
My thoughts than your thoughts."
ISAIAH 55:9 SKJV

Hiking a wooded trail is both energizing and relaxing. And coming into a large meadow or open field can be truly exhilarating, as we see the breadth of nature spread out before us.

The grass, flowers, trees, sky, birds, and butterflies stand out immediately. But what we don't always realize is that we're viewing an ecosystem teeming with life—in the air, on the ground, and under the surface. Not just plants, birds, and butterflies, but thousands of species of insects, fungi, and other life forms fill the outdoors.

If we could strip away everything that hinders our view, we'd be amazed at the scope of life God has created. His creative genius is beyond our comprehension. We could study biology for a lifetime and only scratch the surface of God's world.

He is absolutely worthy of our obedience and praise.

FOR FURTHER THOUGHT

What are your favorite parts of creation? How often do you thank God for what He's made?

How can you share the truth of your creator God with someone who doesn't yet know Him?

PRAYER

Father, I take so much for granted. Slow me down to study Your creation—to praise and thank You for all You have made.

THE WONDERFUL WIND

"The wind blows wherever it pleases. You hear its sound, but you cannot tell where it comes from or where it is going. So it is with everyone born of the Spirit."
JOHN 3:8 NIV

In Hawaii, it's said, you can lean into the stiff winds at the Nuuanu Pali State Park and actually find yourself held up. Though that's a dramatic example, we see the effects of the wind around us all the time—there are gentle breezes that rustle the leaves, howling storms that rattle our windows, and frightening hurricanes that demolish whole buildings.

Jesus said God's Holy Spirit is like the wind—invisible in itself, yet showing powerful effects. What did the Spirit of God do in our lives when we were born again? Hasn't He comforted us in times of trial, helped us when we didn't know how to pray, and given us boldness when we had the opportunity to share the gospel?

And, like the Hawaiian winds, the Spirit also holds us up when we're buffeted by temptation. He even lifts us up to the throne of the Father after we have sinned, so we can confess and receive forgiveness.

FOR FURTHER THOUGHT

What is the strongest wind you've ever experienced? What did you think of it?

How is the Holy Spirit in your life like the wind?

PRAYER

Father, I thank You for Your Holy Spirit who lives within me. Help me to lean on Him and His power.

LEARNING PATIENCE STREAMSIDE

Being strengthened with all power according to his glorious might so that you may have great endurance and patience.
COLOSSIANS 1:11 NIV

The nineteenth-century fly-fishing expert Francis Francis once wrote, "The one great ingredient in successful fly fishing is patience."

An accurate observation, to be sure, if not incredibly obvious to most fishermen.

A person needn't be a sage fly-fishing veteran to know that patience is the one virtue most needed for success. Anyone who has spent any amount of time casting flies—even the *right* fly in the *right* spot—knows there are days when the difference between failure and success is patience.

You have to keep at the work.

The apostle Paul pointed out that living a life pleasing to God—a life of faith—requires endurance and patience too. Those are two virtues God Himself gives, both through the empowerment of His Holy Spirit and by allowing us to go through times that test and strengthen that patience.

Perhaps the easiest way to have that patience tested, strengthened, and refined is when you're enjoying some quiet, relaxing time outdoors.

FOR FURTHER THOUGHT

When has your patience been tested? How did you do?

Who is the most patient person you know? What can you learn from that person?

PRAYER

Lord, thank You for teaching me the virtue of patience—and for doing it while I enjoy my time in Your great outdoors.

STREAMSIDE THOUGHTS OF GOD

The heavens declare the glory of God;
the skies proclaim the work of his hands.
PSALM 19:1 NIV

Those who approach fly-fishing with passion know that a day on their favorite waters can be the very definition of the word *solitude*. It's when anglers spend time alone with their own thoughts—and alone with God.

Some of the most intimate encounters with God recorded in the Bible took place in a wilderness setting. Moses received his calling there. A battered and defeated Elijah took encouragement and strength far away from civilization. And Jesus Himself understood the importance of "getting away" so He could remain in perfect harmony with His Father in heaven.

Someone once observed, "Some go to church and think about fishing; others go fishing and think about God." While a day of fly-fishing should never take the place of regular fellowship and worship at church, it is certainly a great setting for a closer time of communion with your heavenly Father.

FOR FURTHER THOUGHT

What are your favorite memories of being alone with God?

Where do you hear God's voice the clearest? How often can you visit that place?

PRAYER

Heavenly Father, please make me an active part of Your church. And allow me to spend quality time with You—alone—in nature.

SIGNS OF THE TIMES

"You know how to interpret the appearance of the earth and the sky. How is it that you don't know how to interpret this present time?"
LUKE 12:56 NIV

Whether it's true or not, every boater knows the saying, "Red sky at night, sailors' delight; red sky in morning, sailors take warning." We instinctively know we should pay attention to the signs of nature to anticipate what might lie ahead for us.

Jesus used this illustration to communicate a spiritual truth: signs are everywhere that God is at work among us. Our job is to make sure we are paying attention. God's hand can be found in the beauty of a sunset as well as in the joy of interacting with children. It can be sensed in the circumstances surrounding an important decision or in the godly counsel we receive from a friend.

As we go about our daily life and work, we should watch for the signs of God at work around us. He is always working for His people (John 5:17), so let's give Him praise for all He's doing.

FOR FURTHER THOUGHT

What signs of God's working have you seen this week? In the past year?

How aware are you of God's work in your everyday life? How can you become more attuned to His work?

PRAYER

Loving Father, help me to see what You are doing around me—and to give You praise.

THE MIND'S EYE

"I am the good shepherd; I know my sheep and my sheep know me."
JOHN 10:14 NIV

Ever "see something" in the clouds—an elephant, a boat, Abraham Lincoln's profile?

That's because our eyes recognize patterns. In a huge crowd of people, we can recognize the one person we know because our mind remembers the pattern and spatial relationships of a face. We can see those features and know them instantly.

We might recognize a few hundred people by seeing their faces, but God recognizes every single person who's ever lived. Not only does He know us, He's also concerned about us in a very personal way. He understands our struggles and celebrates our joys.

God knows us so well that He even knows how many hairs we have. Nobody on earth knows so much about another person, no matter how much love he might feel for her.

How much God cares for us individually is beyond the reach of our imagination.

FOR FURTHER THOUGHT

Who do you know best in this world? What level of detail do you remember of that person?

Does it comfort you to realize God knows you better than anyone else does? Why or why not?

PRAYER

Lord, let me know my value in Your eyes.
I want to appreciate how much You love me.

LONGING TO KNOW MORE

"I did not believe their words until I came and my eyes had seen it. And behold, half the greatness of your wisdom was not told to me, for you exceed the report that I heard."

2 CHRONICLES 9:6 SKJV

When you see beautiful photos of a place you've never visited, what goes through your mind? Probably not, *Well, I've seen the pictures, so I guess that's enough.* More likely you'd think, *This is gorgeous. I'll have to go there and see it for myself!*

Photos and documentaries of far-off places pique our interest, setting up a longing to travel. But as a picture of a hamburger doesn't quiet the rumbling in our stomach, neither do these beautiful pictures satisfy our wanderlust.

When the queen of Sheba heard about King Solomon's greatness, she wasn't content to stop there. She had to see it for herself—and she was impressed indeed.

Luke 11:31 (SKJV) tells us that "something greater than Solomon" is here. May the glory of our Lord Jesus Christ create a longing to know Him more.

FOR FURTHER THOUGHT

What places on earth would you like to see again, or for the first time?

What about Jesus would you like to know better? How can you fulfill that desire?

PRAYER

Lord Jesus, I long to know You more. Please reveal Yourself to me through Your Word, through Your creation, and through my interactions with Your people.

WHICH WAY TO CHOOSE?

Altogether, Enoch lived a total of 365 years. Enoch walked faithfully with God; then he was no more, because God took him away.

GENESIS 5:23–24 NIV

In a particular city park, you'll find an area where hiking trails diffuse into a small network of interconnected paths with a single entry point and a single exit. Standing at the entry point, trying to determine which path to take, is confusing—even when you realize they all end in the same place.

The Christian life is a lot like that. We're faced with choices—both small and large—every day. In each year of our lives, we stand at the beginning with only a vague idea of the countless decisions that lie ahead of us.

Enoch chose to walk closely with God every day of his 365 years. We can choose his pathway for the next 365 days of our lives. Take the challenge to walk closer with God every day. He'll never disappoint you.

Choosing to put God first makes all the other choices of life easier. Why wouldn't we do that?

FOR FURTHER THOUGHT

Do you find it hard or easy to put God first in your everyday life? Why?

Can you think of a time when you put God first? What difference did that make?

PRAYER

Father, please help me to choose You each and every day. I want to travel the right path—Your path.

DELIVERED FROM TEMPTATION

The Lord knows how to deliver the godly out of temptations.
2 PETER 2:9 SKJV

Fly fishermen understand something about temptation. Most serious fly fishermen carry boxes and boxes of flies—of different colors, patterns, and sizes—because they know that an ordinarily wary, selective trout is likely to give in to temptation and take at least one of those good-looking flies.

Like the fly fisherman who knows what it takes to tempt a fish, our spiritual enemy, the devil, knows well what it takes to tempt us into sin. And the best fly fisherman has nothing on the devil when it comes to presentation. Satan will lay a terrible temptation in front of us, making it look harmless—but hooking us and persuading us to do things that we know are displeasing to God.

The "good news" side of this story is that God knows well how to keep us from temptation. If we look to Him for strength, He's more than willing to protect us from harm.

FOR FURTHER THOUGHT

When have you faced temptation that looked harmless but was far from it? What was the outcome?

Are there any verses or Bible stories that help you to resist temptation? Are you willing to search out others?

PRAYER

Father, thank You for using something as simple as fly-fishing to show me Your vigilance to deliver me from the temptations of this world.

DO NOT WAVER

The one who doubts is like the surf of the sea, driven and tossed by the wind.

JAMES 1:6 NASB

With the crack of the bat, the outfielder raced forward. Then, suddenly, he backtracked. Quickly he adjusted again, racing toward the plate.

By the time he decided where the ball was headed, it dropped harmlessly in front of him. What should have been an easy out turned into a bases-clearing double that put his team behind.

The ballplayer had been fooled.

That can happen in the Christian life too. We go back and forth, sometimes fearing that a strong stand for God is somehow overbearing. But wavering just makes us look unstable. We're tossed around like a wave in the wind.

Doubt does that to us. Today let's make the decision to believe completely in God and His Word. Let's take a firm stand and follow Jesus.

FOR FURTHER THOUGHT

When have you found yourself doubting the goodness of God? What has helped you to trust Him more?

Why are we tempted to doubt God? What negative influences might you avoid?

PRAYER

Father God, please bolster my faith today. May I plant my feet firmly on You.

A STEP IN FAITH

Your word is a lamp to my feet and a light to my path.
PSALM 119:105 SKJV

A hiker caught in the hills after nightfall will tell you there's nothing like the darkness of the countryside—especially if the night is cloudy. Without the benefit of street lighting, the moon, or the stars, it can be difficult to see your own hand in front of your face.

On the great "hike" of life, we can blunder into a similar plight. Souls that stray from Christ may feel that same smothering darkness, spiritually speaking.

Out on the trail, a flashlight, a map, and a compass make it possible for us to walk for miles and arrive at our destination, regardless of the time of day. In the Christian life, we have a map and compass in God's holy book, the

Bible. And, as for a flashlight, well, we have Jesus Christ, the light of the world.

FOR FURTHER THOUGHT

How often do you allow the Bible to guide you along life's paths? Why do we sometimes *not* do that?

What is a favorite verse that helps you in the "hike" of life?

PRAYER

Lord, I can't always see where I'm going. Please help me to keep faith as I step into the unknown. Bring me safely home at journey's end.

RESTING AND RECREATING. . .IN PEACE

"Peace be with you!"
JOHN 20:26 NIV

Ask some people why they enjoy spending weekends in the outdoors, and they'll tell you it's so they can enjoy a little peace and quiet.

There is something truly soothing, relaxing, and refreshing about being in the wild. It's good for the soul to be away from the noise of home, away from the distractions life brings, away from the busyness of the everyday. Nature is where you hear the rushing of water rather than rushing traffic, the singing of birds rather than the voices of people arguing, the sounds of nature as God created it rather than the sounds of human "civilization." These are the places where you can be alone with your thoughts and with your God. . .in total, uninterrupted peace.

A lot of men spend a lot of time in the outdoors without really knowing what they're looking for. But for those of us who spend that time with God, we know we're seeking the peace that only God can give.

FOR FURTHER THOUGHT

What is your favorite place to find peace and quiet? How often do you get to enjoy that place?

How can you find peace when you're not in a natural locale?

PRAYER

Thank You, God, for giving me peace—Your peace! Thank You too for giving me natural settings in which I can fully enjoy that peace.

GOD SPEAKS THROUGH THE EVERYDAY

The desert and the parched land will be glad; the wilderness will rejoice and blossom. Like the crocus, it will burst into bloom; it will rejoice greatly and shout for joy.

ISAIAH 35:1–2 NIV

When you're outdoors enjoying your favorite activities, do you take time to listen to God? It's a great idea, because God has a way of using what we understand to teach us things we haven't yet grasped.

From the beginning of time, He has employed what His people were most familiar with to illustrate His love for them. Jesus continued that heavenly tradition when He described everyday, "outdoor" things the people of His time could understand—the birds of the air, the lilies and grass of the field—to teach them not to worry (Matthew 6:25–34).

As you participate in your favorite outdoor activity, listen for God's voice. It just might be that He'll use something as commonplace as a bird, a flower, or the movement of the wind to lovingly speak His truth to you.

FOR FURTHER THOUGHT

When have you heard God's voice when you were out in nature? What speaks most to you when you're outdoors?

What issues are troubling you at the moment? When can you get away for some quiet time with God?

PRAYER

Lord, thank You for giving me what we call "nature" to help me understand so many of Your other gifts—physical, emotional, and spiritual.

LESSONS FROM THE WILDFLOWERS

"And why do you worry about clothes? See how the flowers of the field grow. They do not labor or spin. Yet I tell you that not even Solomon in all his splendor was dressed like one of these."

MATTHEW 6:28–29 NIV

Have you ever stopped to consider the beauty and simplicity of the wildflowers—those cheery plant faces that grow so peacefully on either side of a hiking trail, or by the river's edge, or on the mountainsides?

There's a great life lesson to learn from every one of those flowers: they grow independently of any self-effort.

Wildflowers don't exert their own energies to grow or blossom so beautifully—and they don't worry about when or how they are to bloom. They just do what they do, simply because that is what God designed them to do.

Next time you're out hiking, fishing, or just enjoying the beauty of nature, take a moment to notice the wildflowers. In many ways, they live a life like the one God wants us to live: one of peace and rest in Him.

FOR FURTHER THOUGHT

What is your favorite flower or plant? How closely have you studied and considered that aspect of God's creation?

What does it say to you that Jesus Himself noticed and appreciated simple things like wildflowers?

PRAYER

Thank You, Lord, for using something as commonplace as a wildflower to teach me not to worry. Help me instead to cast all my cares on You.

EARTHLY PARADISE. . . MADE PERFECT

He made known to us the mystery of his will according to his good pleasure, which he purposed in Christ, to be put into effect when the times reach their fulfillment—to bring unity to all things in heaven and on earth under Christ.

EPHESIANS 1:9–10 NIV

It's probably safe to say that most Christians who've enjoyed the natural beauty of God's created world have also found their thoughts directed toward heaven and eternal perfection.

We Christians can enjoy the wonders of the created world—but we also know the biblical truth that what was once "very good" was thrown into chaos when sin entered the Garden of Eden.

There are wonderful promises, though, in God's written

Word. One day all things will be restored to their original state of perfection.

Imagine for a moment your very favorite places on earth—places you spend time enjoying the natural beauty God has created for you. Then imagine those places as not only pleasant but absolutely perfect. . .just like you will one day be in Jesus Christ.

FOR FURTHER THOUGHT

How have you seen sin affecting the physical world?

How often do you think of a restored, perfect world? How can you direct your mind toward the goodness God has promised?

PRAYER

Thank You, Father, for Your promise that one day we will live as perfectly redeemed people—and in eternal perfection!

A SENSE OF PEACE

The Lord blesses his people with peace.
Psalm 29:11 NIV

It's probably safe to say that most outdoors people, whatever their favorite activity, have described their time away from everyday life with words such as *peaceful* and *quiet*.

Sometimes we just need to get away from the hustle and busyness of the five- (or six- or seven-) day work week. The outdoors is one place we can truly isolate ourselves from the cares of the "real" world and just enjoy some much-needed relaxation.

King David understood the importance of the peace only God could give him. As the divinely appointed leader of the nation of Israel—serving through some very difficult times—David had plenty to do every day. But he always remembered that God was the one source of true peace in the midst of the noise and craziness life brought his way.

God wants us to understand the very same thing—and He can use our time in the outdoors to give us the inner peace we need.

FOR FURTHER THOUGHT

How can you find peace when you can't get to your favorite outdoor locale?

When has God given you a peace that was beyond understanding?

PRAYER

Thank You, Lord, for giving me the peace only You can give. And thank You for using my time in the outdoors to impart that peace to me.

DEATH IN THE POT

So they poured it out for the men to eat. And it came to pass, as they were eating the stew, that they cried out and said, "O man of God, there is death in the pot!" And they could not eat from it.

2 KINGS 4:40 SKJV

Preparing for a day of wilderness activity, most of us fill our packs with food we're familiar with—sandwiches, trail mix, energy bars loaded with carbs. Unless you're a trained survivalist, you probably don't want to rely on the food available at your destination.

During a famine in Elisha's day, fellow prophets gathered a variety of plants, herbs, and gourds from the nearby fields. But they "did not know what they were" (2 Kings

4:39 SKJV). One swallow told them they weren't in Mama's kitchen anymore.

When we're accustomed to good food, the bad stuff just doesn't cut it. That's true of spiritual food too. If we fill up on the "good home cooking" of scripture, we'll be able to detect when there is "death in the pot" in a world that rejects our God.

FOR FURTHER THOUGHT

What is your favorite food for outdoor adventures? Have you ever run out or had to improvise like Elisha's prophets?

When have you tried to substitute the "food" of this world for the goodness of God? How did that go?

PRAYER

Lord, please fill me with Your goodness so I might reject the bitter taste of this world's fare.

NATURAL REMINDERS OF GOD'S GOODNESS

"I will make rivers flow on barren heights, and springs within the valleys. I will turn the desert into pools of water, and the parched ground into springs."

Isaiah 41:18 NIV

Those of us who've spent time in the "high desert" of the western United States know how a good rain shower can change everything. What had been a dry and dusty land only hours before becomes an area teeming with the sights and sounds of natural life.

These are great moments to enjoy the visual beauty, the sounds, and the smells of nature. It's also a good time to remember the goodness of God.

In the Bible, rain in a dry place is often an illustration of

God coming to His people to bless them—to give to them what they didn't have before or to restore something that had been lost. So when a good shower soaks you in a place that's been dry, let it be a reminder of God's goodness to you.

FOR FURTHER THOUGHT

Have you ever experienced—or at least were aware of—a physical drought? How does the coming of rain affect your mental and emotional state?

What are some of the ways God "rains" His goodness on you?

PRAYER

Father, I thank You for natural reminders of Your willingness to bless me, to do for me what otherwise I can't.

STREAMSIDE HOSPITALITY

Do not forget to entertain strangers, for by this some have entertained angels unawares.

HEBREWS 13:2 SKJV

Most fishermen are friendly folks, easily approached even when they're enjoying their pastime. That can change, though, if you ask an obviously successful angler what kind of bait, lure, or fly he's using.

For whatever reason, some anglers are reluctant to share their secrets of success—as if clueing in others will diminish their own take of fish. But it should never be that way for followers of Christ, those of us Jesus commanded to fish for people as well.

The Bible commands believers to be hospitable to everyone, to give to those who have needs, and to take advantage of every opportunity to tell others about God's love.

So when you're asked to share the reason for your success with another fisherman, do it cheerfully. You never know—you might just open a door to telling him about the love of God.

FOR FURTHER THOUGHT

How hospitable would you say you are? How might you become more hospitable?

Have you ever been asked to share the reason for your faith? Was it easy or hard to answer? Why?

PRAYER

Lord, remind me to always treat those I meet with hospitality and godly love.

BE A STEWARD OF NATURE

Then the LORD *God took the man and put him in the Garden of Eden to cultivate it and tend it.*
GENESIS 2:15 NASB

Words like *conservation* and *preservation* can be tricky. Too many people want to take them too far, treating nature as an object of worship.

But it's also possible for people—Christians included—to give them too little consideration. We might feel that the world is temporal and therefore doesn't need to be treated with great care.

The psalm writer David sang, "The earth is the LORD's, and everything in it" (Psalm 24:1 NIV). That biblical truth takes on a deeper meaning for those of us who enjoy resting and recreating in the outdoors. We realize that natural resources are not our own but God's.

The Lord created the mountains we climb, the forests we hike through, the streams and lakes we fish, and everything else we have the privilege of using for outdoor recreation. He always intended for us to "cultivate and tend" them.

FOR FURTHER THOUGHT

What does it mean that God has created natural resources for us to "cultivate and tend"?

What can you do to conserve and preserve the outdoors?

PRAYER

Lord, help me never to forget that I am a steward and a caretaker of the outdoor resources You created.

SPIRIT TO SPIRIT

Then the dust shall return to the earth as it was,
and the spirit shall return to God who gave it.
ECCLESIASTES 12:7 SKJV

It takes special equipment for humans to explore the depths of the ocean—and the deeper you want to go, the more sophisticated that equipment becomes. Simply put, human beings were not created to thrive (or even survive) in water.

In a similar sense, we've all been issued special equipment—our bodies—to live here on earth. Take an informal survey, and most people will probably tell you that we are human bodies with a spirit. In reality, we are spirits with a human body. There's quite a difference between the two views.

Our bodies are limited, designed to last a short time.

No matter how well we take care of ourselves, these bodies will ultimately fail. But the spirit? That's a different matter entirely. Let's be sure we're nourishing and exercising it in view of eternity.

FOR FURTHER THOUGHT

How important is it to take care of your body? What does God's Word say about that?

What do you do to nourish your spirit? Why is this even more important?

PRAYER

Lord, help me always to remember that it's my spirit—not this body—that's eternal. May I connect with You from deep within.

MUDBALL

For we are his workmanship, created in Christ Jesus for good works, which God prepared beforehand so that we would walk in them.

EPHESIANS 2:10 NASB

For decades, nearly all professional baseballs have been prepared with Blackburne's Rubbing Mud, taken from a secret location in the Delaware River.

In baseball's earlier years, various leagues tried a number of things to deal with shiny, slippery new balls—mud from the playing field, ashes, shoe polish, even tobacco juice. Nothing worked quite right. Then Lena Blackburne, a coach and former player, discovered the special mud formula. Today every baseball is rubbed down with this important goo before each game.

God seems to prepare His people in the same way. We like to put on a shiny, clean appearance for others, but the Lord has a way of stripping us of all such pretense. Many Christians have been dragged through muddy messes of life before they were just right for the Lord's purposes.

If you have had a fairly easy life, free of major troubles, God can use you. If you have experienced terrible problems—even to the point you considered your life a total mess—God can *especially* use you!

FOR FURTHER THOUGHT

How has God rubbed the "shiny, clean" sheen off your life? Why does He do that?

When have your struggles given you a connection with another person? How did that go?

PRAYER

Lord, please help me to walk in the good works You've prepared for me.

REACH AND ROLL

Now what I am commanding you today is not too difficult for you or beyond your reach.
DEUTERONOMY 30:11 NIV

Unless you're an experienced kayaker, the little boat might look scary. The thought of capsizing—plunging into the cold, blinding rapids and desperately scrambling for the surface—is something many of us would rather not consider.

But watch an experienced kayaker. No sooner does he tip over than he's up again, in a maneuver called an "Eskimo roll." It's practiced in safer waters until it becomes a habit, an instinctive reaction in more perilous moments.

Finding himself upside down, the experienced kayaker will reach out with his paddle, sweep it through the water, and quickly turn upright. How smoothly the whole thing goes depends largely on how far out he reaches.

There's a picture of the Christian life here. None of us can tell when our entire lives might flip upside down—and we risk drowning if we don't know what to do. But if we've practiced reaching out in those quieter, safer times, we'll be able to roll with the trials.

Let's reach out for Christ in the good times—and when trouble comes, we'll soon find ourselves upright again.

FOR FURTHER THOUGHT

What life circumstances have proved frightening to you? How quickly did you reach out to Jesus?

How can you prepare now for the spiritual and emotional capsizes to come?

PRAYER

Lord Jesus, my arms are short—but Yours encircle the world. When I reach for You, please set me right!

ON RAPPEL!

Now faith is the substance of things hoped for, the evidence of things not seen.
HEBREWS 11:1 SKJV

The overhanging cliff at Whitesides Mountain, North Carolina, is 720 feet high. When you're hanging on a rope halfway down, it's too late to check the knot. The only thing you can do is have faith in the person who tied that knot. And the person who sewed the rappelling harness. And the person who ran the machine that made the rope. . .

Stuck in midair, we can't see any of those people or be sure of their skill. Sometimes we're convinced the knot won't hold—and we're going to die. But to panic is to die; having faith is the only way to live. All we can do is hold on to the rope.

The Old Testament prophets couldn't see their Messiah, but they believed. More than two thousand years later, we can't see our Messiah directly either. Thomas required proof, but Jesus said, "Blessed are those who have not seen and yet have believed" (John 20:29 SKJV). You want to be blessed, right? Just believe.

FOR FURTHER THOUGHT

How easy or difficult is it for you to believe in someone you cannot see? Why?

Why do you think the Bible includes the story of Thomas? How well can you relate to him?

PRAYER

Creator of mountains and cliffs, grant me the strength to hold on to Your rope. . . and the faith that it will bear my weight.

IN A TIGHT SPOT

To You they cried out and they fled to safety;
in You they trusted and were not disappointed.
PSALM 22:5 NASB

You're on a smooth rock face, hundreds of feet up. You need a handhold if you're going to go any farther, but there just isn't one to be found. There is a crack in the rock but very little to grip. What to do?

Here's where you call on a friend. That's the affectionate name for a piece of climbing equipment also known as a spring-loaded camming device. Slip it into a tight space and it expands, gripping the rock. Then you can attach a carabiner, slip your safety rope through it and relax. Even if you were to fall now, your "friend" would catch you.

We as Christians have a friend for every tight spot in

which we find outselves. Jesus makes a better anchor than any camming device. Let's trust our safety to Him and breathe a sigh of relief, knowing that He'll never let us fall.

FOR FURTHER THOUGHT

Can you think of a time you called on Jesus to help you out of a tight spot? What was the outcome?

How easy or hard is it to trust in Jesus' aid? Why?

PRAYER

Lord, the things of this world all fail—
and I am part of this world myself. May I
trust only in You to catch me when I fall.

BRING A FRIEND

"In the same way your Father in heaven is not willing that any of these little ones should perish."
MATTHEW 18:14 NIV

Divers often operate on what they call the "buddy system." Each one is responsible for the safety of another. Generally, they use no more than a third of the air in their tanks on each dive. Should something go wrong, one will have enough air to get both of them back to the surface.

Divers don't need their "buddy" to be a close friend—any fellow diver will do. It's good for us as Christians to be willing to serve our fellow man in the same way.

As children of God, we know He is the Father of all who believe in His Son, Jesus Christ. So the next time you see one of His kids—or yet-to-be kids—in trouble, put the buddy system into effect and help that person come home. God isn't willing that anyone should perish, you know.

FOR FURTHER THOUGHT

When have you needed a buddy to help you come home to the Father?

When have you had an opportunity to be that buddy for someone else? How did it work out?

PRAYER

Father God, I know that You want as many people to know You as possible—in fact, all heaven celebrates when a person is saved. Give me the courage to invite everyone around me to find their way home.

OUR HELPER IN TROUBLE

God is our refuge and strength,
an ever-present help in trouble.
PSALM 46:1 NIV

From a campsite facing a bare rock wall, a father and his three kids began an adventure.

The climb wasn't too difficult. Each person gripped the edges of slabs and wedged fingers in cracks to make their way upward.

At the top, though, Dad had some second thoughts. Going down the same way seemed dangerous—a forty-foot fall to the broken rocks below wasn't his idea of family fun. So he prayed.

Deciding against an immediate descent, the four walked along the ridgeline. Soon, old gnarled trees gave way to a thicket of young saplings among stumps. Evidence of a logging operation meant there must be an old skid road nearby!

Dad and the kids found the safe path, descending at a comfortable walk—and praising their helper in troubles.

FOR FURTHER THOUGHT

When have you asked God to show you which path to take—on a hike or in life? How did He answer?

How consistently do you request God's guidance? How can you be even more quick to seek His way?

PRAYER

Thank You, God, for showing me the way of life—for both my body and my soul.

THE SMALL THINGS MATTER

"Who dares despise the day of small things, since the seven eyes of the Lord that range throughout the earth will rejoice when they see the chosen capstone in the hand of Zerubbabel?"

Zechariah 4:10 NIV

The lake seemed pretty tame. The growth around it was marshy and unremarkable. The water itself was brown and lackluster. It wasn't large enough for boating or skiing. There was really nothing exciting about the place.

But a group of boys thought otherwise. The smooth, flat stones nearby were perfect for skipping across the water. Branches pulled from the bushes on the shore became battleships on the sea. The boys even conjured up schemes to capture the elusive creatures that hid among the reeds.

We adults can learn a lot from kids. Too often, we go through life not even noticing the scenery. Sometimes we cave in to grumbling over another "boring day." But God reminds us to pay attention to the small things—the way children do.

Today, let's ask God to open our eyes to see what He sees—at our workplace, at our church, or in our home. God loves the things He's created, and He wants us to enjoy the thrill of discovering them.

FOR FURTHER THOUGHT

Can you think of a time you overlooked something that was small but consequential? What happened?

How can you tune your senses to God's "small things," whether they're physical or spiritual?

PRAYER

Lord, please open my eyes to appreciate Your small wonders around me.

THE CENTURY

Forgetting what is behind and straining toward what is ahead, I press on toward the goal to win the prize for which God has called me heavenward in Christ Jesus.

PHILIPPIANS 3:13–14 NIV

Ambitious bicyclists pursue "the century," a single-day ride of a hundred miles.

Aspirants prepare with a weeks-long training program. On the big day, they pack high-energy foods like grains, nuts, and fruits, along with plenty of water for proper hydration. Anticipation soaring, they pedal off to bicycling glory.

But for many, there's a "bonk," also known as "hitting the wall." Maybe they started too fast, forgot to eat or drink soon enough, or just weren't in as good of shape as they thought they were. Somewhere along the line, the century gets tough.

That's a lot like life. No matter how strong we think we are, there's often a bonk. It might be a physical problem, a troubled relationship, a nagging temptation. . .but it's real, and it's hard.

The apostle Paul's advice? Don't stop. Keep moving—straining, even—toward Jesus, the goal of your heavenly century. You can do it!

FOR FURTHER THOUGHT

What is the greatest physical challenge you've attempted? How did it go?

When have you "bonked" spiritually? How did you recover?

PRAYER

Lord, when the journey gets hard, please help me to stay the course, eyes always on You.

OUR HELMET

Therefore, take up the full armor of God, so that you will be able to resist on the evil day, and having done everything, to stand firm. . . . And take the helmet of salvation.

EPHESIANS 6:13, 17 NASB

Yes, that outdoor safety equipment is meant to be used.

Imagine a kayaker slipping laterally against a roaring waterfall. For an instant, he hangs there, supported by his paddle against the plunging water. Then the paddle is ripped from his hands and the kayak rolls beneath the water!

A life jacket protects the kayaker's body but not his head. Surfacing after a full 360-degree roll, he sees his helmet strapped to the front of the boat and thinks, *That's a really stupid place for a helmet,* before being dragged down again into the roiling foam. Finally, he escapes downriver.

A helmet protects our brains. . .but it's useless until it's worn. This is truth in the spiritual realm as well. Never, ever leave your full armor behind.

FOR FURTHER THOUGHT

Have you ever left your safety equipment—your armor—at home? How did things turn out?

When have you been unprotected spiritually? How did that go?

PRAYER

Lord, I thank You for providing me with full spiritual protection—help me remember to wear every piece of it.

INGENUITY AND IMPROVISATION

Jesus said to him, "I am the way, the truth, and the life. No man comes to the Father except through Me."

JOHN 14:6 SKJV

Few of us pursue the brand of adventure embraced by television's *Survivorman*. Carrying his own cameras, Les Stroud spent seven days in a hostile wilderness, without food, shelter, fresh water, or tools, relying on his own ingenuity and improvisation to live.

But Stroud's experience pales in comparison with that of James Lovell, Jack Swigert, and Fred Haise, astronauts of the Apollo 13 mission. On April 13, 1970, an explosion aboard their moon-bound spacecraft critically limited power, heat, and water, some two hundred thousand miles from home. The ingenuity and improvisation of the NASA team, both aboard the crippled craft and at Houston's mission control, averted a horrifying disaster.

We human beings take pride in our ability to adapt and adjust, to find ways of overcoming tough situations. But on the biggest challenge of all, bridging the gap between our sinful selves and the perfect, holy God, we're completely powerless. Only Jesus can do that, no matter how much ingenuity and improvisation we try to bring to bear.

We must simply accept the life He offers.

FOR FURTHER THOUGHT

When have you relied on your own strength and know-how to survive an ordeal? What happened?

When have you relied on God's strength for a challenge? How did that turn out?

PRAYER

Jesus, Savior, may I rely completely on Your strength and goodness—never my own.

SAFEGUARDING OUR STUFF

"Behold, I come quickly. Hold fast what you have, that no man takes your crown."
REVELATION 3:11 SKJV

In some places, campers need to take extraordinary care to safeguard their food from hungry wildlife.

Park rangers have shown visitors photos of the aftermath of a bear's attempt to get food from parked cars. Windows were smashed and seats ripped, the food containers thoroughly ransacked. You can just imagine a full-bellied bear whistling happily through the woods afterward.

Campers are advised to store their food in tight containers, even to elevate them by a rope tied to a branch. And since the leftovers attract beasts too, several parks use specially designed waste containers to keep the wildlife out.

It's all about protecting what's inside.

On the spiritual level, let's protect what *we* have inside. We've all seen how the "predators" of life can get inside us and ransack our peace. Look ahead at your day's itinerary; then say a prayer for God to guard your heart and the treasure within.

May nothing ever take our supplies—or our heavenly crown.

FOR FURTHER THOUGHT

What is the best way to safeguard your heart? How consistently are you doing that?

When have you been tempted to leave your spirit open to predators? How did that play out?

PRAYER

Lord God, I want my spirit to be safe—
may I always keep myself within Your protective care.

ANCIENT PATHS

This is what the Lord *says: "Stand at the crossroads and look; ask for the ancient paths, ask where the good way is, and walk in it, and you will find rest for your souls."*

Jeremiah 6:16 NIV

Ever hiked some woods you'd never been in before? If so, you probably stuck to the paths that hikers before you had followed, and from which they had presumably returned home safely.

There's a comfort in knowing that others have paved the way and lived to tell about it. It sets our mind at ease, allowing us to fully enjoy our surroundings.

That's the message God spoke to Israel through the prophet Jeremiah. The Lord had already set His people on a certain course many generations before—and He wanted the present generation to travel those ancient paths too. God told them that if they would do so, they would find rest for their souls. They could have—but they refused.

How do you view the "old ways"? Do they appear archaic and boring? They probably seemed that way to the people Jeremiah spoke to as well. Don't resist the ancient paths. Walk in them and find rest.

FOR FURTHER THOUGHT

When have you been lost, either outdoors or while traveling in a new place? How did that feel?

Do you like or dislike the idea of God's "ancient paths"? Why?

PRAYER

Father, show me Your old paths today and help me to walk in them.

BONDS OF FRIENDSHIP

A man who has friends must show himself friendly,
and there is a friend who sticks closer than a brother.

Proverbs 18:24 SKJV

On a bank of central Oregon's Deschutes River, near a camping area fishermen know as "Mecca Flat," is a small tree, surrounded at its base by chicken wire. In front of the tree, a short piece of rebar holds a sign reading, "In memory of an old fishing buddy." Hanging from the post is a rusty old coffee can, which fishermen use to dip water out of the river for the tree, in memory of fishing buddies who have passed on.

During the dry season, plant life around the little tree turns brown and brittle. But thanks to the help of its "friends," the tree itself remains green and vibrant all summer long.

Outdoor adventures give us a chance to enjoy one of God's great blessings: the bonds of friendship with others who enjoy the same activities. Each time we head outdoors, let's remember to thank God for the "partners in adventure" He's given us.

FOR FURTHER THOUGHT

What friends have you made while enjoying outdoor adventures? What has sustained those friendships?

Who is the "friend who sticks closer than a brother"? How well do you know Him?

PRAYER

Thank You, Lord, for using outdoor activities to strengthen the bonds of friendship I enjoy with the people You've brought into my life.

TRAINING FOR THE TOP

Now Abishai, the brother of Joab, the son of Zeruiah, was chief of the thirty. And he swung his spear against three hundred and killed them, and had a name as well as the three.

2 Samuel 23:18 NASB

With sweat-streaked muscles gleaming in the sunlight, a man crossed the finish line of his first Ironman triathlon. As he slowly sank to his knees, he pumped his fist in a sign of personal victory.

He hadn't won the race, but he'd finished. The previous year he had focused almost exclusively on this moment. The dedication and sacrifice to become one of the few who could successfully complete the course had been enormous. With a finish under his belt, the goal now became to win.

What are your goals? Are you focused on becoming a top athlete, a successful business executive, a published author? Great! Go for it.

Here's the bigger question: Are you focusing the same kind of energy and dedication on becoming a man of God? That's even better. Yearn for it. Train for it. Go for it.

FOR FURTHER THOUGHT

What is your favorite form of physical challenge? How hard do you pursue it?

How hard do you pursue spiritual growth and development? How could you up your game here?

PRAYER

Lord, help me today to focus on becoming the best person I can be—in Your strength.

PURE FOREVER

Purify me with hyssop, and I will be clean;
cleanse me, and I will be whiter than snow.
PSALM 51:7 NASB

Snowy landscapes have a pure beauty, free of the unpleasant details of other seasons. The dazzling white stuff that covers the ground hides some less appealing images of warmer seasons—muddy trails, rotting logs, and bugs lie buried out of sight.

Who isn't warmed by scenes of a snug, well-lit home blanketed in snow against the bitter winds of winter? A wisp of smoke from the chimney tells us all is well. The yard displays nothing to spoil the picture of peaceful contentment. Come spring, though, the melting snow may reveal a yard full of trash, broken toys, and weeds.

Let's be thankful that when God clothes us in the righteousness of Christ, He no longer sees our sins—we are whiter than snow in His sight. And, unlike snow, His righteousness covers us forever!

FOR FURTHER THOUGHT

What is the most beautiful place you've ever seen? What made it so?

How pure are you in your own goodness and strength? How does Jesus change that?

PRAYER

Father, I need Your cleansing. I thank You for providing the way for me to be clean in Your sight, through the sacrifice of Your Son.

A GOD WHO CREATES AND SUSTAINS

"I say to you, unless a grain of wheat falls into the ground and dies, it remains alone. But if it dies, it brings forth much fruit."

JOHN 12:24 SKJV

Have you ever considered the spectacle of nature as it undergoes its annual cycle of birth, life, and death. . .then repeats the same process the same way the following year?

Consider, for example, the stone fly. Fly fishermen know that each spring, the stone fly nymph crawls onto dry land, sheds its skin, mates. . .then deposits its eggs back into the river and dies. The process not only ensures another generation of stone flies but provides food for the birds and fish that live near the river—not to mention a great season of fly-fishing.

These things don't happen by chance. The same God who set all things in motion works year-round to sustain them, to bring them back to exactly where they need to be at exactly the right time.

If God cares that much for stone flies, think how much He cares for you!

FOR FURTHER THOUGHT

How much do you think God cares about even the smallest details of your life? How does the story of the stone fly affect your answer?

Why do you think God created you? Why does He sustain you?

PRAYER

Thank You, God, for sustaining Your creation, for keeping all things moving and growing as they have from the very beginning.

ROUGHING IT

She brought forth her firstborn son, and wrapped Him in swaddling cloths, and laid Him in a manger, because there was no room for them in the inn.

LUKE 2:7 SKJV

When it comes to campers, the "roughing it" scale varies dramatically.

Some insist on an intimate connection with nature, eschewing even a tent. A sleeping bag under the stars is quite enough for them.

Others prefer a tent covering but still lie on the ground. An air mattress seems right to some, while others like their tent to "pop up" from a trailer with pullout beds. RVers camp in what are essentially rolling hotel rooms, featuring televisions, refrigerators, and showers.

Mary, soon to deliver the baby Jesus, could only dream of a comfortable place to stay. With the Bethlehem inn declaring NO VACANCY, Mary and her husband, Joseph, ended up in a cave or stable—nobody knows for sure, just that there was an animal feeding trough handy. There, in the humblest circumstances, the Creator and King of the entire universe was born as a helpless infant.

Jesus was "roughing it" on earth—dramatically so some thirty years later when He died on the cross for our sins. And aren't you glad?

FOR FURTHER THOUGHT

On a scale ranging from "roughing" it to "glamping," how do you prefer to enjoy the outdoors? Why?

Why would Jesus leave the glories of heaven to live on this earth? How should you respond to that sacrifice?

PRAYER

Lord Jesus, thank You for the sacrifices You made on my behalf.

JESUS CALMS THE STORM

Jesus was in the stern, sleeping on a cushion.
The disciples woke him and said to him,
"Teacher, don't you care if we drown?" He got up,
rebuked the wind and said to the waves, "Quiet! Be still!"
Then the wind died down and it was completely calm.
MARK 4:38–39 NIV

Viewing a large body of water can be an awesome experience. Some resemble a huge bowl of gelatin, without a single ripple to mar the placid surface. Others rage like an angry beast seeking to destroy.

One time the apostles—many of them experienced sailors—were terrified by a storm at sea. All the while, Jesus slept. Don't our lives occasionally seem like that? Things get rough and we wonder if Jesus is sleeping. We want Him to wake up and calm our storms immediately. Otherwise, we fear we'll go down with the ship.

Modern ships are watertight if all the hatches and portals are securely sealed. Our faith is a lot like a ship: Watertight, it protects us from the storm. But with holes in our faith we risk sinking. Stop the gaps by studying God's Word, spending time in His presence, and denying yourself sinful pleasures.

FOR FURTHER THOUGHT

How "watertight" is your faith? What specifically can you do to improve its integrity?

How much time are you spending in Bible study and prayer? How much time could you add to that?

PRAYER

Lord Jesus, help me to realize my ship can't sink as long as You're in it with me.

DRAWING STRENGTH FROM OTHERS

I also told them about the gracious hand of my God on me and what the king had said to me. They replied, "Let us start rebuilding." So they began this good work.

NEHEMIAH 2:18 NIV

In the course of planning a trip, we might be inspired to pore over stories of our destination. And those stories might inspire us to become better people.

Think of the pioneers who crossed the mountains in spite of the terrible wind and snow or the valiant soldiers who contested a battlefield. Stories of past conquests inspire us to imitate those brave men and women who achieved so much. Somewhere, deep in all our hearts, is a desire to rise above obstacles and accomplish great things.

So it was when Nehemiah told the Israelites of God's hand upon him. Inspired by God's goodness and presence, the people strengthened their hearts to rebuild the war-ravaged wall around Jerusalem.

Let the Bible's stories inspire you. Find strength in biographies of people who were moved by God to achieve much. Imitate them—and inspire those behind you.

FOR FURTHER THOUGHT

Who are some of the most inspiring people you've read about? Who are the most inspiring people you've known personally?

How is your life inspiring those behind you? What changes could you make to improve your legacy?

PRAYER

Lord, as You've worked wonderfully in the lives of others, please work in my life too.

HE CAME TO SAVE

"For the Son of Man has come to save what was lost."
MATTHEW 18:11 SKJV

Outdoor adventures have the potential to become dangerous. An unwary backpacker loses his way in the woods. . .a sudden snowstorm blinds a skier. . .an avalanche strands climbers.

When an outdoorsman is in trouble, hunters, skiers, climbers, and other hardy folks often mount a massive search-and-rescue effort. They might march in formation, looking for clues to the lost hiker's whereabouts. They'll scale steep mountain faces to rescue trapped climbers. They soar in helicopters, seeking out the lost. The effort expended is mind boggling—and greatly appreciated by those who need the aid.

We can't even imagine the amount of help God has sent into our world. We see His hand in homeless shelters, crisis centers, hospital visits, church outreaches, and the innumerable volunteers who mop up after natural disasters. He works through everyday people like all of us.

No matter how bad things get, God will be there with the help we need. And then He'll be happy to use us to share that help with others.

FOR FURTHER THOUGHT

When have you needed some kind of physical help? Who showed up to provide it?

How has God provided the spiritual, emotional, or physical aid you've needed? How can you "pay it forward" to others?

PRAYER

Lord, here are my two hands—please show me how I can be part of Your network of aid to the world.

REMEMBER PAST VICTORIES

"And the LORD our God turned him over to us, and we defeated him with his sons and all his people."
DEUTERONOMY 2:33 NASB

Imagine a family taking up kayaking on the river rapids—they don't tackle the most dangerous waters first. (Though Mom might tackle Dad, who came up with this whole crazy idea.)

Wise kayakers consider the "class" of a river before entering the water. Class I waters are easily navigated, while Class VI rapids are considered "unrunnable." Trained guides help less-experienced boaters advance through the levels.

In the spiritual life, God also trains in stages. He often allows us to experience small trials to give us confidence in His faithfulness. As we remember how He's helped us through, we build up hope and trust for the next, potentially larger, trial.

To strengthen the Israelites for coming warfare, Moses reminded them of battles they'd won with the Lord's help. Today, as we're faced with spiritual challenges, let's remind ourselves of past victories too—always recalling the God who guided us through.

FOR FURTHER THOUGHT

What are some of the greatest spiritual challenges you've faced? What was the outcome of each?

How does remembering God's earlier protection and provision help you face new challenges?

PRAYER

Lord, You have been my strength in the past. Now give me strength to overcome the new challenges I face.

PRAISE ON SKIS

"Have you entered into the treasuries of the snow?
Or have you seen the treasuries of the hail?"
JOB 38:22 SKJV

The Nobel laureate Fridtjof Nansen may have been a little tongue in cheek when he said, "It is better to go skiing and think of God than it is to go to church and think of skiing." But he did have a point. A champion skier and skater, and an influential Arctic explorer, Nansen knew about finding God outdoors.

A church building is important. It helps create a sense of community, gives people of faith somewhere to recharge their batteries, and often plays a great role in supporting the hungry and needy. And you can certainly worship God there.

But Nansen knew God was also in the hiss of the snow under his skis, in the chill wind against his cheeks, and in the howl of the distant wolf.

So don't neglect your church attendance—but when you're skiing or playing football or cycling or walking the dog or whatever, think of God while you're doing it. He made it all possible!

FOR FURTHER THOUGHT

What are your favorite outdoor activities? How have you experienced God through them?

Why is church attendance important? How consistently do you take part in a local church body?

PRAYER

Wherever I am, whatever I'm doing, Lord,
I want to praise You for everything.

WALKING NEAR THE EDGE

For You are my rock and my fortress. Therefore for Your name's sake, lead me and guide me.

PSALM 31:3 SKJV

There are few experiences like walking a snow-covered mountain peak. But it comes with certain perils: Sometimes the ground underfoot is treacherous.

Wind can blow snow into a ledge—called a "cornice"—that might extend over a steep drop. So climbers have found it's a good idea to tie themselves to a rock before venturing too near the edge. If there are no rocks handy, a piece of equipment known as a "deadman" (similar to the blade of a small shovel) can be driven into the snow as an anchor. Should they suddenly fall through a cornice, the deadman may well save a climber's life.

In the sinful world we live in, the ground can drop out from under our feet at any moment. But the Christian has an anchor in the most unexpected situations—a dead man who came back to life.

Tie yourself to Christ, and you can go anywhere with confidence.

FOR FURTHER THOUGHT

When have you been in dangerous physical places? How did you protect yourself from them?

When have you experienced spiritual dangers? How did Jesus provide safety?

PRAYER

Jesus, my Savior, guide my feet in the uncertain places of life. Please put me on the firm ground that leads to You.

GOD SEES ALL

"For His eyes are upon the ways of a person, and He sees all his steps. There is no darkness or deep shadow where the workers of injustice can hide themselves."

JOB 34:21–22 NASB

We can spend all day in a forest and see only an occasional chickadee or squirrel. But the morning after a fresh snowfall, we'll probably see evidence of a flurry of activity.

The long strides of a deer show the path it chose in browsing from tree to tree. A straight and steady dotted line of rounded tracks means a fox was intent on reaching some destination—when the line weaves back and forth, he was looking for a meal.

There are little mysteries too. The tiny trail of a shrew seems to stop next to the end of a protruding stick. A closer look reveals, between stick and snow, a gap just big enough for that smallest of mammals to sneak down to a protected world next to the earth.

Tracks in the snow are evidence of what we don't see—and a good metaphor for God's work in our world.

Sometimes we fret about what we do see—the evil and sin that plagues humanity. What we can't see is that God is watching too, and He has complete knowledge of who's hurting other people. And He will deal with it in His time.

FOR FURTHER THOUGHT

What troubles you most about modern society?

How confident are you in God's ultimate justice? How can you patiently trust Him with the resolution of all things?

PRAYER

Lord, I thank You that no one doing evil can hide from Your sight—and that You will deal with each one according to Your righteousness.

SLOW BUT SURE

"I have set you an example that you should do as I have done for you."
JOHN 13:15 NIV

One way to descend a steep, snow-covered slope is to zip up your waterproof suit and launch yourself downhill, face-first, arms by your sides. This human bobsled maneuver is called "penguin diving," and it's great fun—until someone hits a rock.

Alternatively, you could take the lead, examine the terrain, and descend slowly, kicking foot holes in the snow. Others will know your path is safe, and each time they step in your footprints, they'll compact the snow even more, making the trail safer still for the rest.

That's a good picture of Christian leadership. Go for

the "cool, flashy" way, and others will probably follow you—with potentially awful results. But if you want to be a leader worthy of the name, follow Christ. It's not always the popular way, but others will see it's good—and they can follow your footsteps all the way home.

FOR FURTHER THOUGHT

When have you made a quick, reckless decision on some important issue? How did it turn out?

When have you made a slow, thoughtful, prayerful decision on an important issue? How did that go?

PRAYER

Jesus, the devil makes his work seem so attractive. Please keep the true cost of the world's way always in my mind, because Yours is the only way worth following.

ALWAYS KEEPING COUNT

"Even the very hairs of your head are all numbered."
MATTHEW 10:30 NIV

If you ever join an organized outdoor expedition, watch the leaders. Chances are, you'll see them regularly stepping aside and casting an eye on the whole group, their fingers or lips moving. They're counting.

Those leaders might know you personally, or they might be just getting to know you—but that's beside the point. Before setting out, they'll have a *number* in mind: the number of people in the group. That figure becomes an obsession of sorts, something to be searched for and found at regular intervals during the trip. It will only be forgotten when everyone is safely home again.

On a much larger level, God is also keeping track of us.

But He never knows us simply as a number. As God does with the stars, He keeps an overall count while calling us each by name (Psalm 147:4).

That is a God you can trust.

FOR FURTHER THOUGHT

What does it mean to you that God calls you by name?

Why would some people wish that God wasn't keeping track of them? Have you ever felt that way?

PRAYER

Lord, it's easy to get lost in this great, big world—at least that's what we sometimes think. Remind me, Father, that You call us all by name. We are always safe with You.

DON'T LOSE YOUR GRIP!

Therefore let the one who thinks he
stands watch out that he does not fall.
1 CORINTHIANS 10:12 NASB

In the 1545 book *Toxophilus*, Roger Ascham presented what he saw as the essential points of archery: standing, nocking, drawing, holding, and loosing. We would call Ascham's "holding" *aiming*.

Many things have to be done well in directing an arrow to the mark. Our results are best when the essentials become habit.

But it's still easy to miss. The archer only needs to stop aiming before loosing, or to stop holding before he is satisfied with his aim. Changing his stance at the moment of loosing will also result in an errant shot.

The Hebrew and Greek words translated "sin" both literally mean "to miss the mark." It's easy for us to miss the mark if we let our eyes stray from the goal—or if we fail to stand for God's truth. If our aim is perfect but we relax our hold at the moment of temptation, we will miss God's mark.

But when it becomes a habit to obey God, we will rarely miss the mark. We will increasingly hit the target that our Lord has set.

FOR FURTHER THOUGHT

What temptations keep you from hitting God's mark? How can you improve your aim?

Who do you know who seems to live his faith consistently? What can you learn from him?

PRAYER

Father in heaven, thank You for warning me against overconfidence. I need You to keep my focus where it belongs—on You, not myself.

I LOVE MY STUFF

For the love of money is a root of all kinds of evil.
Some people, eager for money, have wandered from
the faith and pierced themselves with many griefs.
1 TIMOTHY 6:10 NIV

You can spend a bundle of money on outdoor equipment and excursions. Whether for the newest satellite technology, the coolest sport clothing, or the best-ever overseas trip, those dollars can run away faster than a startled rabbit.

The Bible never says we shouldn't spend money on our love of the outdoors. But there are some cautionary principles to remember.

Scripture warns of "the love of money" as "a root of all kinds of evil." For most of us, the love of money doesn't mean we stack and admire our coins and bills—we enjoy the *stuff* those coins and bills can buy. And when that stuff pulls us away from God, when we buy it to impress (or worse, *depress*) others, when we allow our spending to interfere with our giving to church or other people. . .then we have a problem.

So enjoy all the blessings God has given you—both the great outdoors and the stuff you use to play in the outdoors. But always beware of that creeping love of money.

FOR FURTHER THOUGHT

How materialistic would you say you are? How would your family or friends answer the question?

What are some ways you can use your money and things to encourage other people to consider Christ?

PRAYER

Lord, please help me to use money and love people—never the other way around.

BEARING UP

You shall guide me with Your counsel
and afterward receive me to glory.
PSALM 73:24 SKJV

Following a compass bearing is relatively easy once you know how. Take a line of sight at the required angle and try to find a clear point in the distance, matching your direction of travel. Walk to that point and take another bearing, continuing the process until you reach your destination.

Open ground is easy to travel, but it's a different game walking through woods, where there are no distant markers. To hold the compass and doggedly follow its arrow doesn't really work, as trees, rocks, and other obstacles force you to deviate from the true direction. All those little turns add up—and you might come out of the woods a mile off course.

God's laws are a lot like a compass. They tell us exactly where we need to go, but sometimes we convince ourselves that bending a rule here or there won't make any difference. The reality is that all those little infractions add up to a lot of trouble.

To reach our destination safely, we need to walk on God's bearing, not our own. After all, He can see above the trees!

FOR FURTHER THOUGHT

When you have lost your way, what has God done to bring you home safely?

How does God help you follow His compass? How willing are you to listen and obey?

PRAYER

Father, sometimes I think I know a lot—but You know everything. Teach me humility and guide me safely home.

IT WAS—AND IS—"GOOD"

God made the wild animals according to their kinds, the livestock according to their kinds, and all the creatures that move along the ground according to their kinds. And God saw that it was good.

GENESIS 1:25 NIV

Our times in the outdoors often present us with some great opportunities to stop and consider the word *good.*

When a fisherman tells you that the fishing is good, that usually means he caught a bunch. When a hunter says the hunting was good, that means that at least a few guys in the party bagged the birds or animals they were pursuing. And when a hiker talks about a good day of hiking, it usually means that nice weather brought an enjoyable day of getting close to the beauty of nature.

When God looked out over His finished creation, He observed that it was "good." Good to look at, good to listen to, good to enjoy as it went about its business of growing and reproducing, just as He designed it to do.

And, of course, it was good for His crown jewel of creation—humanity—to enjoy in every way.

FOR FURTHER THOUGHT

Is it easy or difficult for you to see God's goodness? Why?

What would help you to see God's goodness in your life? Are you willing to pursue that?

PRAYER

Creator God, thank You for Your goodness. And thank You that everything You created for me to enjoy is itself also good.

HOW TO BE A BLESSED HUNTER

If you come across a bird's nest beside the road, either in a tree or on the ground, and the mother is sitting on the young or on the eggs, do not take the mother with the young.
DEUTERONOMY 22:6 NIV

Ancient Israel had hunting laws just like we do today—and for similar reasons. God knew that unregulated hunting would, over time, deplete the wild game population. So, though He didn't explain the reasons for the rule, He told the Israelites to let mother birds go free.

Domestic chickens didn't yet exist in Israel, but God knew the Israelites would enjoy cooking eggs or raising wild birds for meat. He allowed that, yet told the people to let mother birds escape and take only the young, "so that it may go well with you and you may have a long life" (Deuteronomy 22:7 NIV).

It seemed like a small rule—and many Israelites were doubtless tempted to break it—yet God promised that if they obeyed, He would see and bless them for it. Though it's not always specifically stated, blessings are attached to obeying *all* God's rules—and He is always watching.

FOR FURTHER THOUGHT

What seemingly small rules has God set forth that you find hard to obey? Why do you struggle?

Is it comforting or disturbing to know that God is always watching you? Why?

PRAYER

God, please help me to obey You, even in the "small" rules.

OUTDOOR FELLOWSHIP

Not giving up meeting together, as some are in the habit of doing, but encouraging one another— and all the more as you see the Day approaching.

HEBREWS 10:25 NIV

It's safe to say that most people who enjoy the outdoors know that few things strengthen the bonds of friendship like hunting, fishing, hiking, and camping. While society calls times like these "bonding," the Bible refers to them as "fellowship."

Shared adventures in the woods, at the fishing hole, on the hiking trail, and at the campground are some of the best possible times to really get to know someone. Almost as enjoyable is reminiscing about adventures past—and planning for future exploits.

Some outdoor adventures are great settings for times of solitude, for prayer and "alone time" with God. But in addition to regular get-togethers at your local church, they're also great settings for fellowship with your brothers or sisters in Christ.

FOR FURTHER THOUGHT

Who are your best friends in outdoor adventure? Why?

When have your outdoor activities been times of praise and worship?

PRAYER

Father, I thank You for giving me times of outdoor solitude. But I thank You also for giving us the outdoors as a setting for fellowship.

MAKE THE LEAP

Therefore, having been justified by faith,
we have peace with God through our Lord Jesus Christ.
ROMANS 5:1 SKJV

The hardest part of learning to rappel is going over the edge of that cliff. That's when you have to lean out, backward, over the abyss. Everything you have ever been taught tells you it's a bad idea, but you have to do it or you're just sliding down a rope.

Once you get that initial positioning correct, it's surprisingly easy. You might go down in little steps the first time, but soon you'll be flying in great bounds, backward, forward, double-handed, and single-handed. It's a real buzz, and you can't believe you wasted so much time being scared.

Coming from the secular world to faith is like stepping

over that cliff. There will be no shortage of people telling you it's a crazy thing to do. But once you step beyond that and get your initial positioning right, then the exhilaration knows no bounds. You can't help but wonder why you didn't do it before.

FOR FURTHER THOUGHT

What's been the most frightening thing about following Jesus? Why?

How has God helped you overcome your spiritual fears?

PRAYER

Father, I am so glad I took that step. Help me help others to get their "positioning" correct.

THE NARROW WAY

"Enter through the narrow gate. For wide is the gate and broad is the road that leads to destruction, and many enter through it. But small is the gate and narrow the road that leads to life, and only a few find it."
MATTHEW 7:13–14 NIV

In Kentucky's Mammoth Cave National Park, aspiring spelunkers wiggle through spaces as small as nine inches high on the Wild Cave Tour.

But even the Historic Tour, a two-mile underground hike for the general public, features a tight squeeze. Though the cave boasts many large, open spaces—like the Mammoth Dome—the trail at one point narrows to a crack in the rock less than a foot wide. Known by the politically incorrect nickname "Fat Man's Misery," the constricted opening forces tour takers to funnel through one by one.

That's a good picture of Jesus' description of the road to eternal life. Crowds on the wide path to destruction are big and careless, unaware of what lies ahead. The faithful, meanwhile, find themselves gingerly navigating a narrow road toward true life.

Christians are an elite group, but they should never be elitist. Call over to those on the other path, and invite them to join you!

FOR FURTHER THOUGHT

How would you enjoy exploring an unmapped cave? Why?

Why has God made His way "narrow"? What keeps people from following His narrow way?

PRAYER

Lord, please give me the boldness to share this faith that's changed my life.

A TRUSTWORTHY CARETAKER

You care for the land and water it; you enrich it abundantly. The streams of God are filled with water.
PSALM 65:9 NIV

Have you ever stood at the edge of a river or stream and wondered how—day after day, month after month, year after year—the water continues to flow? There are, of course, natural and scientific explanations to the process, but for the follower of Christ, the "process" always comes back to the God who created and sustains all things.

The Bible teaches that God didn't just create the natural wonders we enjoy, then stand back to let them take their own course. No, the same God who made these things works every moment to ensure their continued operation, just as He designed them.

Think for a moment about the God who is able—just by His word—to keep and sustain the rivers, lakes, and oceans we enjoy. How much easier must it be for this loving Creator to sustain *you* in every way?

FOR FURTHER THOUGHT

In what ways does nature turn your thoughts to the creator God?

How confident are you in God's power to sustain you? Why?

PRAYER

Lord, I thank You for showing me Your great faithfulness in sustaining all You have created. I thank You for sustaining me too!

SKYDIVE!

Come near to God and he will come near to you.
James 4:8 NIV

There's no feeling quite like exiting a soaring airplane.

When you jump from a plane moving in excess of one hundred miles per hour, your body moves forward with the plane momentarily. Then you decelerate, and the force of gravity begins pulling you straight down. That moment of deceleration is the closest a person can come to actually flying without the aid of a machine.

As a parachutist begins to plummet toward earth, everything becomes silent. Then the parachute opens, and the built-in "dog door" flaps make a faint sound. This slight noise is the only sound to be heard as the skydiver continues to descend from the clouds.

It's hard to be more alone than at this point of a dive. Though we Christians know we're never truly *alone* because God is always with us.

Use those quiet moments—while floating to earth under a parachute or maybe when you first get into your car for the commute home—to spend with the Lord. There's nothing like being completely alone with Him.

FOR FURTHER THOUGHT

Is it easy or hard to find time to be completely alone with the Lord? Why?

How does being alone with God benefit you? How does it benefit Him?

PRAYER

Lord, during my busy day, help me to find some quiet time alone with You.

THIRSTY FOR GOD

As the deer pants for the water brooks,
so my soul pants for You, O God.
My soul thirsts for God, for the living God.
PSALM 42:1–2 SKJV

Three kinds of deer once lived in Israel—the red deer, the spotted fallow deer, and the roe deer. None of them roam Israel's wilds anymore, but they once were a common sight in her forests and wilderness. As the sun beat down all day, deer became very thirsty. Flowing brooks were few and far between, and the deer knew exactly where they were.

David recognized that he thirsted for God just like the deer that stopped grazing, compelled to seek out a brook to slake its thirst. For David, taking time to "tank up" on God was not simply an obligation or a religious duty—it was a pressing need. He could never be too busy for God.

Thousands of years have passed, and today we live in just as dry and thirsty a world. While many religions and faiths promise spiritual refreshment, there is still only one true source of flowing, life-giving water—our living God.

FOR FURTHER THOUGHT

When have you truly thirsted for God? How did He fulfill that thirst?

What other things offer to slake our spiritual thirst? How fulfilling have you found them to be?

PRAYER

God, I desperately need You. Help me to drink deeply of Your Spirit today.

THRIVING IN THE STORM

Suddenly a furious storm came up on the lake, so that the waves swept over the boat. But Jesus was sleeping.
MATTHEW 8:24 NIV

What outdoors person hasn't, at one time or another, been stuck in the middle of a good old-fashioned rainstorm? We often remember those storms with laughter, recalling how helpless we felt as the water pelted down. Sometimes, however, those storms remind us of the dangers of outdoor life.

Jesus faced the latter kind of storm, the likes of which His disciples—at least four of whom were experienced fishermen—had apparently never seen before. As the rain and wind pounded their boat, they longed for Jesus to do something before they died in the middle of the lake. Jesus, on the other hand, was sleeping soundly.

Jesus could rest like that because He knew that God's plan for Him didn't include dying in a freak storm. What a picture of peace and assurance He provides.

No matter what kind of storm we face, we can rest, just like Jesus did, in the assurance that God knows what's going on—and that He's working to use that storm for our benefit and His glory.

FOR FURTHER THOUGHT

When have you experienced an inconvenient rainstorm? Have you ever been in a dangerous storm?

How can you give every storm—physical, emotional, or spiritual—to Jesus?

PRAYER

Father, I thank You for reminding me that You are with me through even the worst of storms.